D0932182

# The Great Debate:
# Advocates and Opponents
# of the American Constitution

## Thomas L. Pangle, Ph.D.

THE
GREAT
COURSES

PUBLISHED BY:

**THE GREAT COURSES**
**Corporate Headquarters**
**4840 Westfields Boulevard, Suite 500**
**Chantilly, Virginia 20151-2299**
**Phone: 1-800-832-2412**
**Fax: 703-378-3819**
**www.thegreatcourses.com**

# Thomas L. Pangle, Ph.D.

Professor of Government
The University of Texas at Austin

Professor Thomas L. Pangle holds the Joe R. Long Chair in Democratic Studies in the Department of Government at The University of Texas at Austin. Before joining the faculty there he held the University Professorship in the Department of Political Science at the University of Toronto. A 1966 graduate of Cornell University (B.A. and Phi Beta Kappa) and the University of Chicago in 1972 (Ph.D. in Political Science), Professor Pangle has taught at Yale University, Dartmouth University, the University of Chicago, the University of Oklahoma, and the École des Hautes Études en Sciences Sociales in Paris.

He has written numerous books on political and intellectual thought: *Montesquieu's Philosophy of Liberalism*, *The Laws of Plato* (translated with notes and a book-length interpretive study), *The Spirit of Modern Republicanism: The Moral Vision of the American Founders and the Philosophy of Locke*, *The Ennobling of Democracy: The Challenge of the Postmodern Age*, *The Learning of Liberty: The Educational Ideas of the American Founders* (coauthored with his wife, Lorraine Pangle), *Justice Among Nations: On the Moral Basis of Power and Peace* (coauthored with Peter J. Ahrensdorf and named an "Outstanding Academic Title" of 1999 by *Choice* magazine), *Political Philosophy and the God of Abraham*, and *Leo Strauss: An Introduction to His Thought and Intellectual Legacy*. He is the editor of *The Roots of Political Philosophy: Ten Forgotten Socratic Dialogues, Translated with Interpretive Studies*; *The Rebirth of Classical Political Rationalism: An Introduction to the Thought of Leo Strauss*; *Political Philosophy and the Human Soul: Essays in Memory of Allan Bloom* (coedited with Michael Palmer). He was also the political theory editor of *The Encyclopedia of Democracy*. From 1995 to 1998, he was the senior advisory editor of *Books in Canada: The Canadian Review of Books*, and since 1997 he has been the general editor of *The Agora Editions* at Cornell University Press.

Professor Pangle is a member of the editorial boards for *Political Research Quarterly* and *Polis: The Journal of the Society for Greek Political Thought*, and he is also a member of the Advisory Board for the Centre for Liberal Education at Carleton University in Ottawa, the Research Council for the International Forum for Democratic Studies of the National

Endowment for Democracy, and the Council of the North American Chapter of the Society for the Study of Greek Political Thought.

Professor Pangle is a fellow of the Royal Society of Canada and has received several prestigious fellowships including the Guggenheim, Killam-Canada Council, Carl Friedrich von Siemens, Connaught Faculty, and Social Sciences and Humanities Research Council fellowships, as well as four fellowships from the National Endowment for the Humanities. Professor Pangle lectures on a variety of topics related to government and politics. He was invited by the Bavarian Academy of Sciences to deliver the Werner Heisenberg Memorial Lecture in Munich and was a featured speaker at the National Endowment for the Humanities Inaugural Colloquium on the Bicentennial of the Constitution at Wake Forest University in 1984. He also has delivered the Exxon Distinguished Lectures in Human Approaches to the Social Sciences at the University of Chicago, the Thomas J. White Lecture at the University of Notre Dame, the Herbert W. Vaughan Lecture on America's founding principles at Princeton University, and the Plenary Address at the 1989 Association of American Law Schools Annual Meeting. His lengthy teaching career has brought him numerous awards and honors; he is the winner of The Benton Bowl at Yale University for his contribution to education in politics and the Robert Foster Cherry Great Teacher of the World Prize from Baylor University.

# Table of Contents

## The Great Debate:
## Advocates and Opponents
## of the American Constitution

# The Great Debate:
# Advocates and Opponents
# of the American Constitution

**Scope:**

The goal of this course is to illuminate the original foundations of our American civic culture by reenacting the Great Debate, from 1787 to 1788, over ratification of the proposed constitution. We will focus on the most profound intellectual and philosophic levels of the controversy, centered on the competing republican visions held by the proponents of the constitution (Federalists) and their opponents (Anti-Federalists).

Lecture One begins by pointing out how essential such a study is if we are to liberate our minds from taking for granted the goodness of the civic culture that shapes us. We then survey the immediately preceding historical background of the debate and some of the major steps in the ratification struggle. We thus become acquainted with each side and begin to appreciate their commonalities and differences. We focus especially on New York State, where some of the most important arguments were published; above all the famous *The Federalist*, written mainly by Alexander Hamilton and James Madison (under the pen name "Publius") in response to Anti-Federalist papers, especially those written under the pen names "Cato" (probably Governor George Clinton) and "Brutus" (probably Supreme Court Justice Robert Yates).

The Anti-Federalists come to sight as conservatives, attacking the Federalists as dangerously extreme innovators. The most serious ground for this is the Anti-Federalist charge that the proposed constitution is too radical a departure from the traditional principles of classical republican government—the tradition that looks back for guidance to the heroically virtuous form of self-governing community that had characterized the Greco-Roman world. In Lecture Two we clarify what this charge means by discovering the exact signification of "classical republicanism" for Americans during the founding period. On this basis, we proceed in Lecture Three to unpack in detail the republican vision that inspires and animates the Anti-Federalist critique of the proposed constitution.

In Lecture Four we turn to the Federalist counterattack, which opens with a dramatic change in the focus of the debate: Whereas the Anti-Federalists concentrate on domestic republican liberty, the Federalists put the stress on the requirements of national security and foreign policy. It is primarily on this basis that "Publius" argues for the necessity of granting to the central government "unlimited" taxation and military power, applied through direct rule over individual citizens without the mediation of the state governments. The Anti-Federalists retort that granting such powers to the central government is unnecessary, dangerous to liberty, and likely to foster enchantment with imperial glory.

In Lecture Five we see how the argument over national security leads to the gravest challenges that each side addresses to the other. The Federalists not only charge the Anti-Federalists with a refusal to face the stern requirements of international security, but they also deepen their critique by suggesting that at bottom the Anti-Federalists have no alternative to either the proposed constitution or a dismemberment of the United States. Indignantly rejecting this accusation, the Anti-Federalists, in their turn, censure the Federalists as wrongly prioritizing national security over domestic liberty. The Anti-Federalists contend that maintaining the correct priority of liberty over national security requires making state governments the bulwark of what should be a far more confederate constitution. For it is at the state and local levels that free self-government is most fully exercised; powerful state governments can best check and balance the otherwise potentially despotic central government.

In Lecture Six we follow the Federalist reply, and in doing so we see that what in fact is intended by the proposed constitution is a system that makes the central government emphatically predominant over the states. This raises a question dealt with in the following lectures—namely, what does the constitution substitute for state governmental power that insures against oppression by the strong central government?

We begin in Lecture Seven with the elaboration of Madison's cornerstone argument. That argument severely criticizes the small-scale, fraternal ideal of classical republicanism and elaborates in its place a new, historically unprecedented republican ideal. The new ideal is rooted in the concept of an enormous commercial society animated by competition among numerous diverse and antagonistic minority factions and requiring, as well as facilitating, a wholly representative, rather than a participatory, form of government.

Lecture Eight traces the main points of contention in the debate over the nature of representation, as that debate is focused on the question of whether or not the proposed House of Representatives adequately represents the will of the people. In following this debate we gain a more concrete grasp of the opposition between the two sides' rival conceptions of the meaning of "valid representation."

Lectures Nine and Ten articulate the debate over the true meaning of "separation of powers" and whether or not the proposed constitution embodies a proper separation and balance of powers.

A crucial disagreement emerges in the differing estimations of the gravest source of the threat of unchecked power. Whereas the Anti-Federalists discern in the proposed Senate a seedbed of undemocratic elite usurpation, Madison insists that the greatest danger in a democratic republic is from the popularly elected House of Representatives, which can appear to be the sole voice of the ultimately sovereign people. Madison sees the proposed Senate as made up of elder statesman somewhat insulated from popular election and hence a crucial moderating counterweight both to the House and to short-sighted popular passions.

The Anti-Federalist fear of the Senate goes together with worries about the monarchic character of the Presidency. We follow Hamilton's defense of the unitary and unified executive against the Anti-Federalist argument for an executive council.

Nothing disturbs the Anti-Federalists more than what they see as the alarmingly elitist role of the Supreme Court—armed with the unheard of power to invalidate as "unconstitutional" laws duly enacted by the people's elected representatives. In Lecture Eleven we see how this expression of alarm provokes Hamilton's famous argument for judicial review. We see how the full, implicit import of this last argument is illuminated by the Anti-Federalist challenges to it.

Our twelfth and concluding lecture brings out the deep ironies in the one great apparent victory achieved by the Anti-Federalists: the addition of the first 10 amendments, which constitute our Bill of Rights. By closing with this part of the Great Debate we highlight, in retrospect, key strengths and weaknesses in the position of each side. The Federalists successfully defended a marvelously well-designed frame of governmental power, while the Anti-Federalists lacked a convincing alternative proposal. In their critique, however, the Anti-Federalists help us to see what the new constitutional order has had to leave behind (especially of the classical tradition) and alert us to some dangers that lurk in this new order as a result. Above all, they highlight the lack of attention to civic virtue, civic education, and citizen participation among the mass of the populace.

# Lecture One
# Significance and Historical Context

**Scope:** A reconsideration of the Great Debate provokes us to reenact for ourselves some of the most powerful arguments for and against our constitutional order. Such rethinking of the pros and cons of our system runs some risk of being politically destabilizing, but it is necessary for genuine intellectual liberation. We start by becoming acquainted with some of the major figures who we will hear from on each side and with the drama of the ratification contest in which they were engaged. Most important is the struggle in New York State, which provoked the writings of several of the most thoughtful Anti-Federalists (opponents of the proposed constitution) and, in response, *The Federalist* by John Jay, Alexander Hamilton, and James Madison, all writing under the pen name "Publius."

# Outline

I. The goal of this course is to illuminate the original foundations of our American constitutional republicanism.

   A. We will bring back to life the great controversy out of which our Constitution was born so that we can begin to reenact, in some degree, the debates, choices, and arguments made by the founding generation.

   B. We will not be looking at arguments over details of the constitution but rather at the Great Debate between two fundamentally conflicting visions of a healthy republic and healthy republican civic life.

   C. Our focus will be on this profound level of disagreement and debate between those who favored and those who opposed the new constitution.

   D. We will learn that while those who favored the constitution won out, those who opposed the constitution also contributed to an ongoing dialogue that has helped to define and enrich the American political tradition.

**II.** The deepest reason why it is so important that we reenact this old controversy is because Americans live within a cultural horizon in which our constitutional system is largely taken for granted.

    **A.** This is a healthy thing for our political life because this means we have a broad consensus on basic principles, which provides the stability and agreement among citizens necessary for a republic to function well.

    **B.** For the political good, however, we pay a serious price in terms of our genuine intellectual freedom.

        **1.** This consensus means that we are not usually challenged by deep criticism of our constitutional order as a whole.

        **2.** We thus are not impelled to rethink the arguments for the basic principles and goals of our system, which puts us in danger of becoming passive, unthinking creatures of our system.

    **C.** By reenacting the Great Debate, we can begin to recover a perspective from which we can see the system coming into being, in and through the eyes of thoughtful proponents and opponents.

    **D.** To try to understand the debate as it was understood at the time, I am going to quote profusely from the original writings and speeches.

**III.** The first American constitution was created during the Revolutionary War.

    **A.** The Articles of Confederation and Perpetual Union established a confederacy (league of friendship) among the 13 states, each of which retained its sovereignty.

        **1.** Most of the important activities of government were carried out by the individual member states.

        **2.** The central government consisted of a single Congress at which each state could case a single, equal vote, with most matters requiring a majority of nine states.

    **B.** This Congress dealt with four kinds of business.

        **1.** Collective foreign policy and defense.

        **2.** Arbitrating disputes between states.

        **3.** Facilitating interstate and foreign commerce.

        **4.** Legislating for the territories.

**C.** During the three years after the war ended, this confederate system came to appear increasingly inadequate.

    **1.** A fierce outbreak of rabidly partisan politics appeared within the states.

    **2.** There were incidents of mob rebellion, including Shays' Rebellion, which had to be forcibly put down by the state militia.

    **3.** In states where the populist forces obtained control of the legislature, laws were passed that threatened property rights and sound financial management.

**IV.** Under a leadership that included James Madison and Alexander Hamilton, the federal Congress called a special convention to meet in Philadelphia in May of 1787 that was authorized to propose changes in the Articles of Confederation.

    **A.** The convention met in secrecy, which allowed for both a freer exchange of views and suspicion among the populace who awaited the outcome.

    **B.** Instead of abiding by its legally assigned task, the convention went beyond its delegated mission and came forth with a new, unprecedented constitution.

        **1.** The convention appealed to the people as the ultimate fountain of constitutional authority.

        **2.** The proposed constitution was not referred back to the existing federal government or the state governments for ratification or discussion.

        **3.** The convention decided that their product should be ratified by special conventions in each state made up of delegates elected directly by the people; ratification by any 9 of the 13 states would be sufficient for the new constitution to come into effect for those ratifying states.

    **C.** A sizeable proportion of the delegates refused to sign the final document. These Anti-Federalists, as the opponents of the constitution were called, were a diverse group with a variety of objections and supporting arguments.

        **1.** Some were for starting all over again (e.g., Governor George Clinton of New York).

        **2.** Others were more moderate critics who called for substantial amendments prior to ratification, to be drafted in a second convention (e.g., Patrick Henry).

3. A softer opposition called for substantial amendments but did not require them prior to ratification (e.g., John Hancock).

D. Proponents of the constitution called themselves Federalists.
   1. They were more united because they all defended the same proposed constitution.
   2. They published *The Federalist*.
   3. They took rhetorical advantage of the fact that the Anti-Federalist arguments were not united around a single alternative plan.

E. For the first century and a half of our country's history, scholars tended to be overly influenced by the rhetorical strategy of the Federalists and ignored the strength of the Anti-Federalist argument. Scholars have recently come to better appreciate the weightiness and depth of the debate on both sides.

V. Hamilton and Madison's *The Federalist* emerged from the New York State contest.

A. It was in response to Anti-Federalist publications that Hamilton organized and led the writing and publication of *The Federalist*.

B. Though Hamilton wrote about two-thirds of the papers, he enlisted the help of James Madison and John Jay.

C. Seen in their immediate context, *The Federalist Papers* are high-level, political advocacy journalism.
   1. The authors were not writing a treatise or a work of political philosophy but an argument for a specific constitution in a specific time and place.
   2. This makes the arguments of *The Federalist* colored by a partisan, debating spirit that is not always fair to its opponents.

**Essential Reading:**

*The Federalist*, Papers 1 and 38.

Gillespie and Lienesch, eds., *Ratifying the Constitution*, Introduction and Forward.

**Supplementary Reading:**

Goldwin, *From Parchment to Power: How James Madison Used the Bill of Rights to Save the Constitution*, Part 1.

Wood, *The Creation of the American Republic*, Chapter 10.

**Questions to Consider:**

1. How deep is the tension between the political need for consensus on our basic constitutional principles and the intellectual need to rethink the most powerful arguments for and against those principles?

2. Some Anti-Federalists were for rejecting the new constitution entirely and starting afresh at a new convention; others were for amending it at a second constitutional convention; still others were for accepting it on the condition that it be amended by the first Congress. Which of these three positions seems the most prudent and wise, and why? What are the best arguments you can give for each position?

# Lecture One—Transcript
## Significance and Historical Context

My goal in this course is to illuminate the deepest original foundations of our American constitutional republicanism, and to do so by bringing back to life the great controversy out of which our Constitution was born, so that we ourselves can begin to re-enact, in some degree, the debates and thus the choices—and more importantly, the arguments for the choices—that were made by the founding generation.

We won't be looking mainly at arguments over details of the Constitution, but rather at what I call the Great Debate between two fundamentally conflicting visions of what a healthy republic—and healthy republican civic life—should be. Our focus is going to be on this most profound level of the disagreement and debate between those who favored and those who opposed the new constitution. We're going to learn that while, of course, those who favored the Constitution won out, and therefore have made the greatest contribution to our political history and culture, it's nevertheless true that those who opposed the Constitution and lost also have contributed to an ongoing dialogue and fertile self-criticism that has helped to define and enrich the American political tradition.

In other words, by studying the great original debate over the Constitution, we are going to become much more aware of a profound and fruitful set of tensions that lie at the heart of the American political experience.

This spotlights the deepest reason why it is so important that we ourselves re-enact this old controversy; we Americans live within a cultural horizon in which our constitutional system is largely taken for granted as good and reasonable. This is a healthy thing for our political life because this means that we have a deep and broad consensus on basic principles; and such consensus provides the stability and the trusty agreement among the citizens that's necessary for a republic to function well.

But, for this political good, we pay a serious price in terms of our genuine intellectual freedom, because this consensus means that we are not usually challenged by deep criticism of our constitutional order as a whole and we're not thus impelled to rethink for and by ourselves the arguments for the basic principles and goals of our system. That puts us in danger of becoming the passive or unquestioning—and hence somewhat unthinking—creatures of our system.

We're not sufficiently aware of the deep questions or serious doubts that thoughtful people can raise about the basic principles underlying our constitutional system. We're not sufficiently aware that such deep questions and serious doubts were raised among the Founders and that the meaning of our Constitution, with its far-reaching implications, was originally thought through and articulated and elaborated in response to such serious challenges.

We tend not to realize how much our constitutional thinking was forged in and through controversy and thus, in an important sense, draws its intellectual strength from controversy and even invites or stimulates controversy, in the light of the original Great Debate, out of which the fundamental meaning of the Constitution was forged.

By re-enacting the debate at the founding, we can begin to acquire an awareness of all this and thus liberate our minds. We can recover a perspective from which we can see the system coming into being, in and through the eyes of thoughtful proponents and opponents, who did not—because they *could* not—take the system and its basic principles and goals for granted.

By listening to the original critics of the Constitution and by seeing how the defenders are responding to those critics, we will have better access to the age-old, deeply puzzling problems, in the very nature of republicanism, with which our founders were wrestling and trying to solve. We can see precisely what dangers this new constitution was meant to combat and what it was designed to achieve. Also, and equally important, we can see what our constitutional system was not designed to achieve, what alternative concerns and goals of political life were abandoned or subordinated, what costs were consciously paid, what limitations were accepted in opting for this, at the time, new system.

All this means that we have to make the effort to try to understand the debate as it was understood at the time, by the most articulate advocates on each side. To help achieve this, I am going to quote profusely from the original documents, from the original writings and speeches, so that we can hear the very words of the contestants and learn to formulate the issues as they formulated them, listening to and judging between them from the inside, as it were.

Let me start by sketching the immediate historical situation that these writings, which we are going to study, emerged out of and primarily addressed. The first American constitution was created during the Revolutionary War, entitled The Articles of Confederation and Perpetual

Union. This established what the document calls, in Article Three, a "confederacy," or "league of friendship," among the 13 states. Each of which explicitly retained what the documents calls its "sovereignty, freedom, and independence," in the wording of Article Two.

In other words, under this first constitution, the United States was, or were—and in those days, everyone used the plural, which is significant—the United States were exactly what the name, United States, really connotes. If you step back and think about it, it wasn't one consolidated country, but instead, a permanent alliance or union of 13 distinct but kindred independent states. Something more like what we see in today's European Union. Accordingly, under this first constitution, many or most of the important activities of government were carried out by the individual member states ruling over their own populations.

The central or federal government was both simple and very limited in its scope and powers. It consisted of only one major institution, a single Congress. There was no judiciary whatsoever, no separate executive. At this Congress, each state had a delegation that could have as many people in it as they wished, but that cast only a single, equal vote. Most important matters required a super-majority, of nine of these state votes. This Congress dealt mainly with four kinds of business. First and foremost, collective foreign policy and defense, but with practically no union army—the military consisted almost entirely of state militias, which could be requisitioned by the central government for limited time periods. Secondly, the Congress also arbitrated disputes between states. Thirdly, it facilitated interstate as well as foreign commerce. Finally, the Congress was responsible, empowered to legislate for the territories.

Especially during the three years after the war ended—and we must never forget that it was this constitution that led the country to victory in the Revolution, so it had behind it a momentous achievement—but in the three years after the Revolution, this confederate system came to appear to more and more Americans, as increasingly inadequate.

In matters of defense, the confederation seemed too weak; in foreign affairs, irresolute and lacking in a unified voice; in domestic affairs, especially regarding finance and the economy, the confederation seemed fragmented and irresponsible as regards payment of the government debts left over from the Revolution. Most worrisome of all was what was beginning to appear within the states, namely a fierce outbreak of rabidly partisan politics, which exhibited an ominous combination of opposite, but mutually reinforcing, bad proclivities. On the one hand, the radical democratic tendencies of the Revolution had bred a widespread popular distrust of government, and this distrust was being whipped up by demagogic populist leaders who branded the elected legislatures as elitist and oligarchic—a charge that took hold especially among those who felt that they were not sharing in the economic boom that occurred at the end of the Revolutionary War, and that meant especially small farmers who were heavily burdened by debt.

As a result, there were strong movements to limit the power of elected state legislatures, especially by requiring the elected representatives to follow strict instructions set out by the majority of the voters during the time of the election. Still worse, there were also incidents of mob rebellion against the laws. Most frightening of all, in the fall and winter of 1786, there was Shays' Rebellion in western Massachusetts, which was an insurrection by small farmers angered by what they regarded as crushing debt and taxes that had to be forcibly put down by the state militia.

On the other hand, in states where the populist forces did obtain control of the legislature, laws were passed that threatened property rights and sound financial management; sometimes by outright confiscation, and more often by impeding debt collection or instigating inflation, by printing masses of paper money.

The degree of the problems was debated at the time, and has continued to be debated by historians studying the period. But many thoughtful people spoke of a growing crisis, and under the leadership that included James Madison and Alexander Hamilton—especially—the federal Congress finally called a special convention to meet in Philadelphia in May of 1787, to which all the states were invited to send delegations and which was authorized to propose changes or amendments in the Articles of Confederation.

This convention met through the entire summer of 1787 in secrecy. Naturally, while the secrecy of the proceedings allowed for a franker and freer debate and exchange of views, it also aroused a good deal of suspicion amongst the populace outside, who awaited the outcome. When the product was finally disclosed on September 17, 1787, there was amongst much of the populace a kind of collective gasp because the rumors were confirmed, the convention had not abided by its legally assigned task, which was, to repeat, to propose amendments to the existing constitution. Instead, the convention had gone far beyond its delegated mission and had come forth with an entirely new, different, unprecedented constitution. Little wonder that opposition exploded almost immediately.

What the convention did, in effect, was to appeal over the head of the existing constitution and national government or federal government to the people themselves, and over the heads of the state governments to the people in the states as the ultimate fountain of all constitutional authority. The proposed constitution was not sent back or referred back to the existing Congress or federal government. It was not offered to them for their ratification or even for their discussion; and it was not sent to the state governments for their ratification or their discussion. Instead, the convention decided that their product should be ratified by special conventions in each state, made up of delegates elected for that purpose directly by the people; which meant, at the time, a majority of the adult male voters, with eligibility requirements that varied from state to state. In addition, the convention decided that ratification by any nine of the 13 state conventions would be sufficient for the new constitution to come into effect for those ratifying states.

As a practical matter, everyone knew that if this new union was to have much chance of success, the ratifying states had to include the four biggest states: Pennsylvania, Virginia, Massachusetts, and New York. In the last three of which—Virginia, Massachusetts, and New York—there was very strong opposition, especially in New York. The leaders of the opposition included some of the men who had themselves been delegates to the constitutional convention.

Because this proposed new constitution was the compromise product of long, strenuous, and sometimes dangerously bitter debate within that secret hall, and the debates took place under some pretty trying circumstances, which have been best described by one major historian, Forrest McDonald, in the following words: "An average of close to 40 men, most of them obese, crowded into a modest-sized and not well ventilated room for five to seven hours a day, during an intensely hot and muggy summer." So, it's not surprising that a sizable proportion of the delegates wound up refusing to sign the final document. Sixteen of the 55 who attended the Philadelphia Convention did not sign the document.

Among these non-signers were some major figures, who immediately began publishing their strong objections. The delegation from Virginia, the state which was the most populous, wealthy, and powerful at the time, was badly split. Three of the Virginians—including George Washington and James

Madison—signed on as supporters. But, in vehement opposition—saying, in fact, that he would rather cut off his right hand than use it to sign this constitution—was George Mason, perhaps the second most respected Virginian of the time, after George Washington. Mason had authored the Virginia Declaration of Rights of 1776, which was the first American bill of rights, preceding, and influencing, Jefferson's Declaration of Independence and also deeply influencing the declarations of rights in other states. Joining Mason in opposition was Edmund Randolph, the governor of Virginia.

The delegation from New York, the second most populous and powerful state, was even more opposed. Alexander Hamilton was the only one of the three New York delegates who supported the Constitution. His two colleagues, Supreme Court Justice Robert Yates and Speaker of the Assembly John Lansing, walked out of the convention early on, in disgust at what was being concocted. Robert Yates is thought to be the author of one of the most insightful and well-argued sets of essays attacking the proposed constitution, the essays that were signed by the pen-name "Brutus."

Other distinguished delegates at the convention who came out in opposition included notably Luther Martin, who was the attorney general of Maryland and recognized as perhaps America's greatest expert on law and legal theory. John Francis Mercer of Maryland, a distinguished lawyer, a hero of the Revolution, who's probably the author of another of the best sets of oppositional writings, which appeared under the pen name, "A Farmer."

These non-signing delegates were joined by other weighty and eloquent writers and speakers in opposition, many or most of whom wrote anonymously, under pen names, as was the custom at that time. Because of this custom of noble anonymity in published political writings, scholars to this day are uncertain, to varying degrees, as to who wrote, as to what was the authorship of many or most of the Anti-Federalist writings.

These "Anti-Federalists," as the opponents of the constitution were called, were of course a diverse lot, with a wide variety of objections and supporting arguments, and they ranged in the degree of their opposition to the proposed constitution. Some were for rejecting the whole scheme and starting all over again. Perhaps most preeminent among these was Governor George Clinton of New York, supported by his allies Lansing and Yates, who had been the delegates who walked out of the convention; and they were joined by Mercy Otis Warren, perhaps the most gifted woman thinker, poet, playwright, and historian of America at that time.

Then there were other more moderate critics, who called for substantial amendments to this proposed constitution but prior to adoption at a second convention. This was the position taken most eloquently by Patrick Henry, who delivered a series of mighty orations against the proposed constitution in the Virginia ratifying convention.

A similar position was taken in Virginia by Richard Henry Lee, who had been a leader of the Revolution and who, in 1786, was President of the Continental Congress and thus the leading official of the existing United States. Lee is, we think, perhaps the author of one of the most influential and widely read of the Anti-Federalist writings, which were written under the title, *The Letters from a Federal Farmer.*

A third and softer opposition position called for substantial amendments, but not requiring them prior to ratification—amendments to be made by the First Congress; this was the position taken in Massachusetts by those heroes of the Revolution, John Hancock, who was in 1787 the governor of Massachusetts and Samuel Adams, who was in 1787 President of the Massachusetts State Senate. In the Massachusetts ratifying convention, Hancock and Adams began by leaning strongly against ratification. But, eventually, as the debates wore on, these two became leaders in striking a compromise, which allowed a victory for ratification in the Massachusetts Convention, by a very close vote, 187 to 168, but with the recommendation that major amendments be made by the first new Congress under the new constitutional system. This compromised form of ratifying, saying yes to ratification, but saying, "And there should be major changes and amendments made by the First Congress," was followed by several other states; it became a kind of paradigm of a way to get compromised ratification.

Meanwhile, on the other side, the proponents of the constitution, who called themselves the Federalists, were also a varied lot. They too ranged in both the degree of their enthusiasm and the reasons for their support of the proposed constitution. But, there's a massive, twofold difference between the two sides in regard to their degree of unity. First and most obviously, the Federalists were more unified, because they were all defending the same basic document, the proposed constitution, while the Anti-Federalists had no single, unifying, alternative proposal to unite them. Secondly, the opponents, the Anti-Federalists, never produced any single publication that ranks, in depth and breadth, with the great *Federalist* papers, that were written mainly by Hamilton and Madison, which over time have come, justifiably, to obscure the numerous other writings and speeches that were published in 1787 in favor of the proposed constitution.

Now, those supporting the proposed constitution, the Federalists, took rhetorical advantage of the facts that their Anti-Federalist opponents were more scattered in their arguments and didn't have a single alternative plan to unite around. The Federalists exploited this to portray their opponents as more incoherent, more contradictory, more lacking in any constructive vision, than they in fact were. This is especially true of James Madison's treatment of his opponents in *Federalist* Paper 38.

For the first century and a half of our country's history, scholars tended to be overly influenced by this rhetorical strategy of the victors, and hence underestimated or ignored the strength of the Anti-Federalist arguments. Although everyone had to concede that the Anti-Federalists did make a great contribution in forcing upon the Federalists the amendments that form the Bill of Rights, because as we shall see, the idea of a national bill of rights was strongly resisted by the Federalists, led by Hamilton and Madison, at first. They eventually agreed to the idea of a bill of rights only when they saw that they had to, if they were going win ratification and to avoid alienating, from the new constitution, that large minority who had opposed it in the Great Debate. It's a serious question that historians debate, whether if there had been a national referendum the constitution would have passed. It's not at all clear that a majority of the Americans would have voted for it.

But apart from this grudging admission that the Anti-Federalists were chiefly responsible for the addition of a bill of rights, leading 19th- and early 20th-century historians of the founding period, such as John Fiske, George Bancroft, and Andrew McLaughlin, gave insufficient attention to the richness of the alternative republican theory and vision that finds expression in the deepest reservations articulated in the best of the Anti-Federalist writings. Then later, scholarship in the early and mid-20th century was blighted by the predominance of an outlook on history that was championed by Charles Beard, who tended to reductively interpret the theorizing of both the Federalists and the Anti-Federalists as mere ideology, masking and promoting the clash of selfish class economic interests.

Historians of the past half century have been remedying this earlier neglect of the theoretical seriousness of Anti-Federalist, as well as Federalist, thinking, and hence scholars have recently come more and more to appreciate better the weightiness and depth of the debate on both sides. A major goal of these lectures of mine is to profit from and to give expression to this more recent, heightened appreciation of the principle power of the argumentation on both sides in the Great Debate.

Let's focus a little more narrowly in on New York state and its contest, out of which Hamilton's and Madison's great *Federalist* papers emerged. In New York, the opponents of the constitution seized the early initiative. Governor Clinton, joined by his allies, Yates and Lansing, and Mercy Warren, published, starting right away in September of 1787, some very powerful newspaper essays and pamphlets attacking the proposed constitution.

It was in response to this Anti-Federalist onslaught that Alexander Hamilton decided he had to organize and lead the writing and publication of *The Federalist Papers* in newspapers. There's a deep sense in which it was the New York Anti-Federalists who provoked and made necessary and thus possible, the greatest commentary on the Constitution's underlying meaning.

Hamilton himself wrote about two-thirds of these famous *Federalist* papers, but he enlisted the help of James Madison, who was visiting New York at the time and who wrote some of the most important papers; and also John Jay, who was later to become the first chief justice of the United States, who, unfortunately, however, was wounded and ended up writing only five of the 85 papers.

Hamilton was also the leading pro-ratification spokesman at the New York ratifying convention, which met the next summer, where there was an eventual Federalist victory, by a very close vote of 30 to 27, on the very late date of July 26, 1788. But this ratification, like that in Massachusetts, included a call for no less than 33 amendments to the constitution, to be enacted by the first Congress.

In Virginia, which ratified in June, the vote was not quite so close, 89 to 79. But it also included a call for 20 amendments, in addition to a Declaration of Rights.

In New York, it was only the arrival of the news of the Virginia ratification, which took a month by horseback to get to New York, which turned the tide. It persuaded a handful of Anti-Federalist delegates, led by Melancton Smith, to switch sides from opposition to grudging acceptance and endorsement of ratification on the grounds that well, if Virginia's going to be in this thing, it would just be too dangerous for New York to stay out.

Seen in their immediate context, *The Federalist Papers* are a very high level, political advocative journalism. A "newspaper discussion," as Hamilton calls them in Paper 11. Hamilton and Madison don't claim to be writing a treatise or a work of true political philosophy. Instead, they're arguing, like good lawyers, for a specific constitution in a specific time and place, against specific opponents. The opponents are these Anti-Federalists, who have published already and continue to publish their writings. This makes, of course, *The Federalist Papers* colored by a partisan, debating spirit that's not always fair to the opponents. Yet, on the other hand, Hamilton and Madison are keenly aware that any argument for a specific kind of government, if it is to be cogent and convincing, must give some well-reasoned response to the most serious objections of the adversaries, especially objections of a fundamental, principled kind. In this case, the opponents have raised grave doubts as to whether the proposed constitution conforms to the basic, traditional, American principles of freedom and republicanism.

The Anti-Federalists charged from the beginning that this proposed constitution represented a dangerously innovating departure from great traditional Republican principles. The principles that have been handed down for generations, that Americans have heretofore made the foundation of their civic life. The principles that carried us through the Revolution, they said, are being abandoned by this document.

The Anti-Federalists thus tend to speak as conservatives, decrying the reckless radicalism of the Federalists and their new constitution. The Federalists respond by, in some measure, proudly accepting the mantle of innovators.

In the next lecture, I want to enter into the serious issues of the Great Debate by starting from this contrast and unpacking what is implied in this apparent conservatism of the Anti-Federalists and the apparent radicalism of the Federalists.

# Lecture Two
# Classical Republicanism

**Scope:** The Anti-Federalists attack the proposed constitutional order as departing too much from the traditionally revered Greco-Roman ideal of virtuous participatory republicanism. We familiarize ourselves with the specific meaning of the classical republican ideal for Americans in the 18$^{th}$ century as rearticulated by the most authoritative political philosopher of the age, Montesquieu. We then clarify the ways in which the Anti-Federalists indicate key reservations against classical republicanism, even as they appeal to it. The Anti-Federalists share with the Federalists, and with Americans of the time generally, a republican vision that is much less communal, and much more individualistic and commercial, than the classical ideal.

## Outline

I. The Anti-Federalists speak as conservatives whereas the Federalists speak as innovators.

    **A.** The Anti-Federalists argue that there is no need for a completely new constitution to replace the existing one, though they do readily acknowledge that the Articles of Confederation need substantial revision.

        **1.** The Anti-Federalists call for some enhancement of the powers of the central government under the Articles.

        **2.** They insist, however, that the basic idea of the existing constitution—its underlying federal principle—is essentially fine.

        **3.** The limitation and balancing of powers, they charge, is lost sight of in the proposed new constitution.

    **B.** The Federalists, in contrast, stand for abandoning the existing constitution and its basic federal principles in order to substitute something dramatically different and unprecedented.

    **C.** Against this kind of thinking, the Anti-Federalists tend to argue that the chief source of the present trouble is not mainly the bad design of the existing constitution but rather a decline in civic and moral spirit among the American people in the years since the

Revolution—the Anti-Federalists see the proposed constitution as doing little to remedy this moral decline and likely to contribute to making it worse.

**D.** This Anti-Federalist stress on the importance of civic virtue signals the more profound level of the conservative stance of the Anti-Federalists.

**1.** They charge that the proposed constitution is too great a departure from age-old, classical principles of republican government.

**2.** In reply to this charge, the Federalists show themselves to be proud radicals in that they acknowledge that their proposed republic *is* without precedent in human history, which signals that their proposed new republic will not have the vices that have always haunted republican governments in previous times and places.

**II.** The proposed constitution's departure from major traditional principles of republicanism brings into focus the issues raised in the Great Debate concerning the nature of sound republicanism, republican liberty, and self-government.

**A.** In *Federalist* 9, we find an unabashed condemnation of the great principles of classical republicanism, the heroically virtuous form of self-governing community that characterized the Greco-Roman world. This severe attack was continued by Madison in *Federalist* 10 and by both Madison and Hamilton in *Federalist* 16–20.

**1.** Classical republicanism had an awesome significance for everyone at the time of the founding.

**2.** Among Americans and Europeans in the 18th century, the most authoritative model of republicanism was the Greco-Roman experience of self-government, the legacy of which had often been invoked during the American Revolution as a source of inspiration and guidance.

**B.** The continuing weight of this classical republican heritage is seen throughout *The Federalist* by virtue of the fact that the authors sign every paper "Publius" (the name of one of the two leading founders of the Roman republic).

**1.** This kind of noble anonymity was very common practice among both Federalists and Anti-Federalists.

**2.** Papers and essays were signed by pen names such as "Brutus," "Cato," "Candidus," "Centinel," and "Cornelius."

C. The original understanding of classical republicanism was available to Americans through the classics of ancient political theory by such philosophers as Aristotle and Cicero, and through the great classics of ancient history such as the works of Thucydides, Plutarch, and Livy.

D. The classical republican tradition had been given its most compelling recent reformulation by the French political philosopher Montesquieu in *The Spirit of the Laws*.
   1. Published in 1748 and immediately translated into English, it was the most important work of political philosophy at the time and was frequently cited as an authority among Americans at the time of the founding.
   2. Montesquieu not only restates the classical republican tradition, but he also reinterprets that tradition and gives to the classical republican experience a new analysis.

III. Montesquieu's reinterpretation profoundly changed the meaning of the classical republican model, giving classical republicanism a meaning that is significantly different from the meaning that it had for the original Greco-Roman thinkers.

A. In its original form, republican government had been understood more in aristocratic than democratic terms.
   1. Republics at their best were understood to be shaped by and for an elite dedicated to wise and heroic civic virtue.
   2. The aristocracy's economic basis was not commercial but instead inherited farming.
   3. The supreme goal of politics was understood to be the exercise of public and private virtues as the highest purpose of the community.

B. Practically, the classical theorists recognized that in almost all actual situations this noble aspiration had to be compromised both to win the necessary support of the rich and to gain the support of the poor and middle classes.

C. The best practical republic was conceived in classical theory as a mixed regime—a republic that combined aristocracy with some democracy by taking considerable power out of the hands of the moral elite and placing it in the hands of the majority of the populace.

1. In the best version of this compromise, the distinguished few had to share power with the ordinary people and govern with their consent without becoming mere servants of the people.

2. The great challenge to the moral elite was to resist the ordinary people's tendency to debase virtue into something regarded as a mere means to popular prosperity, liberty, and security.

**D.** In a Christianized version, this classical conception had been the dominant political outlook of the New England Puritans, who were a cornerstone of the American republican tradition.

**E.** Montesquieu, in contrast, argued that the true virtues of the classical republics were more egalitarian; he contended that the classical republic, at its best, was democratic rather than aristocratic.

1. Such a democracy must be small enough so that the people can assemble and so that those who stand for election are familiar to, resemble, and remain under the close scrutiny of the rest of the populace.

2. Montesquieu stressed that a true democracy requires in all its ordinary citizens an intense public spirit.

3. A chief business of such a democratic community is legislating this moral ethos, requiring that all citizens conform to the ethos of egalitarian, communal civic virtue (which requires a single established religion).

**IV.** The classical republican ideal in both its original version and the version of Montesquieu was held in high honor by the Anti-Federalists—who appealed to key elements of Montesquieu's version as a standard by which to judge and condemn the proposed constitution and its unclassical underlying vision of republican life—but it was not unreservedly embraced by them.

**A.** The Anti-Federalists speak of the chief goal of government as being the securing of rights and liberties in an individualistic and libertarian sense.

**B.** The Anti-Federalists share with the Federalists a vision of America as being larger in scale than any classical republic, more commercial and economically growth-oriented, and more individualistic and liberal.

**C.** What most distinguishes the Anti-Federalist republican outlook from the classical republican ideal is that the Anti-Federalists tend to see politics as less a positive good and more a necessary evil required to protect the personal liberty of individuals who exercise their liberty largely in more private pursuits.

**D.** The Anti-Federalists are unclassical in the degree to which they are apt to see government and participation in politics as intrinsically corrupt because humans are, by nature, prone to use power to seek more power.

**E.** On this basis of a very qualified appeal to classical republicanism, the Anti-Federalists opposed the new constitution.

    **1.** They saw the proposed constitution as threatening individual rights and freedoms by excessively centralizing governmental power and by removing government too far from the direct control of the citizens.

    **2.** What is needed instead, in the Anti-Federalist view, is a true confederacy of smaller, localized, more classical, and more participatory democracies.

**Essential Reading:**

"Cato" [probably George Clinton], 3rd letter; in Storing, *The Complete Anti-Federalist*, Vol. 2, pp. 109–13.

*The Federalist*, Papers 9 and 14.

Mason, speech at the Virginia Ratifying Convention (June 4, 1788); in Storing, *The Complete Anti-Federalist*, Vol. 5, pp. 255–59.

Montesquieu, *The Spirit of the Laws*, Book 2, Chapters 1 and 2; Book 3, Chapters 1–3; Book 4, Chapters 4–8; Book 5, Chapters 1–7; Book 7, Chapters 2 and 8–16; Book 8, Chapters 2, 3, and 16.

Turner, speeches at the Massachusetts Ratifying Convention (January 17 and February 6, 1787); in Storing, *The Complete Anti-Federalist*, Vol. 4, pp. 217–21.

**Supplementary Reading:**

Storing, *What the Anti-Federalists Were For*, Chapters 1 and 2.

**Questions to Consider:**

1. What are the most important ways in which the classical model of democracy, as restated by Montesquieu, differ from the democracy we are familiar with today?

2. In what respects do the Anti-Federalists embrace and depart from the classical idea of democracy as articulated by Montesquieu?

# Lecture Two—Transcript
## Classical Republicanism

As we saw at the end of the last lecture, a massive first impression we get is that the Anti-Federalists, or opponents of the proposed constitution, speak as conservatives, whereas the Federalists, or defenders of the proposed constitution, speak as innovators.

This is true most immediately and obviously in that the Anti-Federalists argue that there is no need for a completely new constitution to replace the existing constitution, though they readily acknowledge that the Articles of Confederation do need some substantial revision. The Anti-Federalists call for some enhancement of the powers of the central government under the Articles. But, they insist, the basic idea of the existing constitution, its underlying truly federal principles, are essentially fine, embodying a properly limited idea of the central government's powers, maintaining a true balance of power between the central and the state governments, and among the state governments. This limitation and balancing of powers, they charge, was lost sight of in the proposed constitution. As the Anti-Federalist speaker Gilbert Livingstone said, in the debates in the New York Ratifying Convention:

> True it is, sir, there are some powers wanted, to make this glorious compact complete. But, sir, let us be cautious that we do not err more on the other hand, by giving power too profusely, when, perhaps, it will be too late to recall it.

The Pennsylvania writer who calls himself "A Federal Republican," commenting on the clause in the proposed constitution which gives to Congress the power to, as our documents says, "levy and raises taxes … to provide for the common defense and general welfare," says:

> Our situation taught us the necessity of enlarging the powers of Congress for certain national purposes, where the deficiency was experienced. Had these and these only been added, experience itself would have been an advocate for the measure. But in the proposed constitution there is an extent of power in Congress, of which I fear neither theory nor practice will evince the propriety or advantage.

The Federalists, in contrast, stand for abandoning the existing constitution and its basic federal principles in order to substitute something dramatically different and unprecedented.

In the words of Hamilton, in *Federalist* Paper 23, "There is an absolute necessity for an entire change in the first principles of the system."

Against this kind of thinking, the Anti-Federalists tend to argue that the chief source of the present troubles is not mainly the bad design of the existing constitution, but rather, a decline in civic and moral spirit among the American people in the years since the Revolution. Thus, Samuel Adams, or a follower of his perhaps, writing under the pen name "Candidus," says, "We are too apt to charge misfortunes to the want of energy in our government, [misfortunes] which we have brought upon ourselves, by dissipation and extravagance." The Anti-Federalists see the proposed constitution as doing little to remedy this more important moral decline among the people and likely to make things worse.

This Anti-Federalist stress on the importance of civic virtue in the populace signals the more profound level of the conservative stance of the Anti-Federalists. They charge that the proposed constitution is too great a departure from age-old, classical principles of republican government. In reply to this charge, the Federalists show themselves to be proud radicals, in that they proudly acknowledge that their proposed republic is of a dramatically new kind, without precedent in human history. What's more, Madison and his allies dare to argue that precisely the innovativeness of the proposed constitutional republic is a good argument for it, because this signals the fact that this new type of republic will not have the vices that have always before haunted republican governments in all previous times and places.

As Madison puts it in Paper 37, when he's beginning to give an overview of the whole new proposal:

> The novelty of the undertaking immediately strikes us. It has been shown, in the course of these papers, that the other confederacies which could be consulted as precedents, have been vitiated by erroneous principles, and can therefore furnish no other light than that of beacons, which give warning of the course to be shunned, without pointing out that which ought to be pursued.

It's this aspect of the proposed constitution, its departure from major traditional, agreed-on principles of republicanism that I want to focus on, first and foremost. Because this will bring into focus what are the deepest issues in the Great Debate, issues concerning the very nature of sound republicanism, republican liberty, and self-government.

A good starting point is what we see leaping out at us from the start of Hamilton's ninth *Federalist* paper. For there we find an unabashed and sweeping condemnation of the great examples and principles of classical republicanism, that heroically virtuous form of self-government that had characterized the Greco-Roman world in its best and most famous moments.

> It is impossible [Hamilton writes] to read the history of the petty republics of Greece and Italy, without feeling sensations of horror and disgust at the distractions with which they were continually agitated, and at the rapid succession of revolutions by which they were kept perpetually vibrating between the extremes of tyranny and anarchy. ... If momentary rays of glory break forth from the gloom, while they dazzle us with a transient and fleeting brilliance, they at the same time admonish us to lament that the vices of government should pervert the direction, and tarnish the luster of those bright talents and exalted endowments for which the favored soils that produced them have been so justly celebrated. ... If it had been found impracticable, [Hamilton goes on] to have devised models of a more perfect structure, [than those ancient Greek and Roman republics,] the enlightened friends to liberty would have been obliged to abandon the cause of that species of government as indefensible.

This severe attack on the classical republican tradition is continued by Madison in the next, tenth, paper, and carried still further by both Madison and Hamilton in Papers 16 through 20, as well as elsewhere.

To grasp the bold character of this attack on the classical tradition, we have to recognize the awesome significance, for everyone at the time of the Founding, of classical republicanism. Among Americans as well as Europeans in the 18th century, the most authoritative model of republicanism in previous history was the Greco-Roman experience of self-government, whose legacy had often been evoked during the Revolution as a source of inspiration and guidance. Thus, for example, in the depths of the terrible winter at Valley Forge, George Washington had rallied morale by having Addison's great tragedy of the Roman hero Cato presented to the starving, freezing troops. Throughout his life, Washington spoke of deep inspiration by the Roman republican models of heroic leadership.

Washington was by no means exceptional in this. Almost everyone in the 18th century, especially in America, agreed that there had been a flowering of republican self-government and civic virtue in classical antiquity. A flowering which loomed as a kind of heroic standard for all succeeding ages.

The continuing weight of this classical republican heritage is seen throughout *The Federalist Papers* by virtue of the fact that the authors sign every paper "Publius," invoking, over and over and over, 85 times, the name of one of the two leading founders of the Roman republic, Publius Valerius Publicola, a hero celebrated in one of Plutarch's famous biographies. This kind of noble anonymity, submerging oneself as an author behind a pen name taken from some classical republican figure, was very common practice among both Federalists and Anti-Federalists. As we proceed, we will be quoting repeatedly papers and essays signed by pen names such as "Brutus," "Cato," "Candidus," "Centinel," "Cincinnatus," "Cornelius," and so forth.

Yet even while Hamilton and Madison embrace this common practice, and thus signal that they do share, to some extent, in the common respect for the classical republican tradition. They soon unveil, as we have now seen from Paper 9, their radical break with that tradition, and thus provoke some of the Anti-Federalists' deepest worries about the proposed new constitutional system.

To understand all that is at stake in this Federalist break with classical republicanism and the deep worries this break arouses in the Anti-Federalists, we have to familiarize ourselves with what was the rich and complex meaning for Americans in the 18th century, of this classical republican tradition. The original understanding of classical republicanism was available to the Americans through the great classics of ancient political theory, written by philosophers such as Aristotle and Cicero, and through the great classics of ancient history, such as the works of Thucydides and Plutarch and Livy.

But as Hamilton reminds us in this same ninth *Federalist* paper from which I read a moment ago, the classical republican tradition had been given its most compelling recent formulation by the great French political philosopher Montesquieu, in his masterpiece *The Spirit of the Laws*, published in 1748, and immediately translated into English. *The Spirit of the Laws* quickly became the most important work of political philosophy of the time and was the work of political philosophy that was the most frequently cited as an authority among Americans at the time of the Founding.

Montesquieu in his masterpiece didn't simply restate the classical republican tradition. In important ways, he reinterprets that tradition. He gives to the classical republican experience a new analysis, and if we're to grasp the complexity of what the classical model meant for Americans at the Founding, we first need to understand precisely how Montesquieu's reinterpretation profoundly changes the meaning of the classical republican models. What exactly then is the key difference between Montesquieu's reinterpretation, reanalysis, and the original analysis provided by the classical philosophers themselves of their work?

In its original form, in the political theory elaborated in the writings of the great Greco-Roman political philosophers and historians, republican government had been understood more in aristocratic than in democratic terms. Republics, at their best, were understood to be shaped by and for an elite, but not an elite defined by or aimed at money or wealth. Instead, an elite genuinely dedicated to wise and sometimes heroic civic virtue, generously preoccupied with a politics of caring for the welfare of the whole community, a welfare defined more in spiritual than in material terms. Thus an elite which conceived of its highest task as that of leading the community in cultivating a refined life of the mind, centered on public, communal religious worship and celebration and reflection, in great public religious festivals, such as produced the magnificent Greek and Latin tragedies and comedies.

This aristocracy's economic basis was not commercial or business or banking, but instead inherited farmland and farming, property of a kind that affords leisure without tempting to acquisitiveness or materialistic love of money.

The life of virtue led by civic leaders was understood not only, or even mainly, as a life of service to the community, to the people. The supreme goal of politics was understood to be neither the promotion of the interests of the rich, with their property and wealth, nor the promotion of the ordinary person's desire for security and liberty and prosperity. Instead, the exercise of the public and private virtues was conceived as itself the highest end or purpose of the community. The life of virtue, civic and intellectual, was held to be itself the peak of human flourishing and the purpose of the best republican community.

Yet as a practical matter, the classical theorists recognized that in almost all actual situations, this high and noble aspiration had to be compromised, both in order to win the necessary support of the more materialistically minded commercial and business rich people and in order to gain the consent and support of the numerically powerful poor and middle classes. In practice, it was understood, the concern for virtue or human excellence has to be diluted by concerns for wealth, freedom, and equality. So the best practical sort of republic was conceived in this classical theory as what was called a "mixed regime," meaning a republic that mixes or combines aristocracy with some democracy by taking considerable power out of the hands of the moral elite and placing that power in the hands of the majority of the populace.

In the best version of this compromise "mixed regime," the few of distinguished virtue had to share power with the many ordinary people, and govern with their consent. But, it was hoped, without becoming the servants of the people. In the mixed regime, the great challenge to the moral elite was to resist or to try to elevate the ordinary people's tendency to debase virtue into something regarded not as the end, but rather as a means, a mere means, to popular prosperity and liberty and security.

Now, in a Christianized version, this original classical conception had been the dominant political outlook of the New England Puritans, who were a cornerstone of the American republican tradition. In a more secular version, the classic mixed regime is articulated by Thomas Jefferson in a famous letter to John Adams written near the end of their lives. For he speaks as follows:

> I agree with you [he writes to Adams] that there is a natural aristocracy among men. The grounds of this are virtue and talents. … There is also an artificial aristocracy founded on wealth and birth, without either virtue or talents. … The natural aristocracy I consider as the most precious gift of nature for the instruction, the trusts, and government of society. … May we not even say [he writes to Adams] that that form of government is the best which provides the most effectually for a pure selection of these natural aristoi into the offices of government? The artificial aristocracy is a mischievous ingredient in government, and provision should be made to prevent its ascendancy. … I think the best remedy is … to leave to the citizens the free election and separation of the aristoi from the pseudo-aristoi, of the wheat from the chaff. In general, they will elect the real good and wise.

Now Montesquieu, in contrast to all this, had argued that the true virtues of the classical republics were more popular, egalitarian—"mediocre," as he put it. Montesquieu contended, against Aristotle and Cicero and Thucydides and Plutarch, that the classical republic at its best was democratic rather than aristocratic. At its best, Montesquieu insisted, the classical republic put supreme power in the hands of the assembly of all the citizens, meeting frequently, to pass by majority vote the fundamental laws and to serve as mass popular juries in court trials and thus to control the judiciary, and also to elect, and later to pass judgment on, administrative officers, who were understood to be the people's public servants.

Such a democracy, Montesquieu pointed out, must be small enough so that the people can assemble and, more importantly, small enough so that those who stand for election to office are familiar to, and resemble, and remain under the close scrutiny of, the rest of the populace.

Even more important than smallness of size, Montesquieu stressed, a true democracy requires in all its ordinary citizens an intense public spirit. Each and every citizen must be willing to devote considerable time and energy and expense to public service, to long meetings, to elaborate discussions, to important committee work, and so on. Montesquieu calls such "virtue" in the people the very "principle," as he puts it, or the "spring" of democracy. Montesquieu explains that this democratic virtue requires among the citizens a deep spirit of kinship or fraternity. Such genuine fraternity requires a homogeneity in the way of life of the inhabitants. Only persons, he argues, who share the same education, the same family mores, the same economic status, the same religion, can look upon one another with an authentic sense of brotherhood and sympathy and empathy. So virtue, he argues, is the love of equality, meaning the love of like for like, the love of and for a society that prevents sharp class distinctions or pronounced diversity.

A chief business of such a democratic community, he argues, is legislating this morality, this moral ethos. Meaning, requiring through all sorts of social pressures, including coercion, and constant moral education of adults as well as children, requiring all citizens to conform to the ethos of egalitarian, communal civic virtue. This requires a single established religion, uniting the society spiritually.

The classical republican ideal, especially in its new Montesquieuan democratic version, was held in high honor, especially by the Anti-Federalists, who appealed to key elements of this Montesquieuan version of the classical ideal as a standard by which to judge and condemn the proposed constitution and its very unclassical underlying vision of republican life.

But, I must hasten to add, the classical republican ideal, even in its newer, more democratic, Montesquieuan version, was not simply or unreservedly embraced by almost anyone in America in 1787, including the Anti-Federalists. It's this deep ambivalence about the classical republican ideal that makes the Anti-Federalist outlook so complicated. Sometimes, to be sure, leading Anti-Federalists do speak in very classical-sounding terms—as when the Anti-Federalist writer who calls himself "Brutus" says in his 7th essay, "We ought," he says, "to furnish the world with an example of a great people, who in their civil institutions hold chiefly in view, the attainment of virtue, and happiness, among ourselves."

But it's more characteristic of the Anti-Federalists, including "Brutus" himself, to speak of the chief goal of government as being the securing of rights and liberties in an individualistic and even what we today might call libertarian sense; meaning, rights and liberties for individuals to pursue their own private happiness as each wishes, especially through the acquisition of more and more private property, through commerce as well as farming, free from governmental, or communal, supervision and interference.

In other words, the Anti-Federalists share with the Federalists a vision of America's future that would be unlike the classical ideal, in that they envisage the future country as being much larger in scale than any classical republic, much more commercial and economically growth-oriented, and much more individualistic, liberal or even libertarian. Yet the Anti-Federalists continue to think, at the risk of some deep inconsistency, that precisely in order to protect this more individualistic liberty, major aspects of the classical ideal need to be preserved and fostered. Aspects that would be abandoned or lost in the constitutional order proposed by the Federalists, they fear.

What most deeply distinguishes the Anti-Federalist outlook from the classical republican ideal, in both its original and its new Montesquieuan form, is that the Anti-Federalists tend to see politics as less a positive good, less an attractive field for moral fulfillment, and more a necessary evil required to protect the personal liberty of individuals who exercise their liberty largely in more private pursuits, especially the pursuit of economic gain. What's more, the Anti-Federalists are un-classical in the degree to which they are apt to see government and participation in politics as intrinsically dubious and even corrupting, because they see humans as by nature very prone to use whatever power they have to seek more and more power. Power likely to be used to exercise exploitative control over others.

As the writer who calls himself "John DeWitt" puts it, "The more we examine the conduct of those men who have been entrusted with the administration of governments, the more assured we shall be ... that mankind have perhaps in every instance abused the authority vested in them, or attempted the abuse." "Brutus" issues a similar judgment, "based," he says, "on the lessons of the Old Testament."

Precisely on the basis of this un-classical degree of distrust of leaders or elites in politics and government, the Anti-Federalists think that the classical ideas of the need for civic virtue in the populace, amongst ordinary citizens, and the need for direct popular participation in government and the need for government to be kept close to and dependent on the people, under their direct, local, popular control, are all essential, to prevent what will otherwise be a steady drift toward oligarchic or aristocratic oppression by whatever elite hold the government offices. As the writer who calls himself "Centinel" puts it, in his first letter:

> A republican, or free government, can only exist where the body of the people are virtuous, and where property is pretty equally divided; in such a government the people are the sovereign, and their sense or opinion is the criterion of every public measure; for when this ceases to be the case, the nature of the government is changed, and an aristocracy, monarchy, or despotism will rise on its ruin.

The Anti-Federalists are concerned, then, for the classical republican ideals of citizen virtue and popular participation in and control over government, not in the way the classics themselves were. These virtues are not seen chiefly as good for their own sakes or as ends, but instead mainly as means to, as necessary protections and supports for, more individualistic rights and freedoms, freedoms of a largely non-political, commercial, and private kind.

It's on this basis, of a very qualified appeal to classical republicanism, that the Anti-Federalists oppose the new constitution. They're worried above all because they see the proposed constitution as threatening individual rights and freedoms by excessively centralizing governmental power, making it too unified and unchecked, and by removing government too far from the direct local control of the people as citizens, making the constitution likely to foster an elite, aristocratic government that would more and more intrude, with domineering effect, in people's lives, with the people becoming more and more like servile servants, rather than active, independent power sharers.

What's needed instead, in the Anti-Federalist view, is maintaining a true confederacy of smaller, localized, more classical and participatory democracies. Thus George Mason expostulates,

> The very idea of converting what was formerly a confederation to a consolidated government, is totally subversive of every principle which has hitherto governed us. ... It is ascertained, by history, [he says] that there never was a government over a very extensive country without destroying the liberties of the people: history also, supported by the opinions of the best writers, show us that ... popular governments can only exist in small territories. Is there a single example, [he challenges the Federalists] on the face of the earth, to support a contrary opinion? ... Was there ever an instance of a general national government extending over so extensive a country, abounding in such a variety of climates, etc., where the people retained their liberty?

Now, in the next lecture, I want to elaborate more fully the rather complex republican vision for America that the Anti-Federalists advocate, showing more concretely exactly how the Anti-Federalists draw upon and adapt and integrate key elements of the classical ideal, and then I'll turn to begin laying out the Federalists' answer and response.

# Lecture Three
# The Anti-Federalists' Republican Vision

**Scope:** The Anti-Federalists contend that, precisely in order to protect individualist rights and liberties, substantial ingredients of the virtue-centered classical republicanism remain essential. We trace the character of the republican vision of the Anti-Federalists by considering their distinctive views on moral and religious legislation; on the importance of local, participatory democracy; and on representative government. All this dictates a constitution that is more decentralized (a system in which state and local governments remain more powerful) than in the more consolidated national government proposed by the Federalists. We introduce the Federalist response, highlighting the way in which the Federalists dramatically shift the focus from internal policy to the demands of national security and foreign policy.

# Outline

I.  The Anti-Federalists make a qualified appeal to the classical republican heritage but contend that, in order to protect individual rights and liberties, substantial ingredients of the old classical ideal in its democratic reformulation must remain essential.

II. The Anti-Federalist position is vividly illustrated by what they say regarding religion.

   A. Anti-Federalists are committed to individual religious freedom yet assume that the religious diversity would and should be a Christian diversity and are convinced that Protestant Christian piety and religious education are essential foundations for civic virtue and citizenship education.

   1. Without a widespread belief in God, too many people are tempted to neglect their demanding civic duties for the sake of pursuing material interests.

   2. Benjamin Franklin, in a major speech on June 28 at the Constitutional Convention, pleaded unsuccessfully for the Convention to return to the prayerful piety that had helped inspire the American Revolution.

**B.** Anti-Federalists warn that the proposed constitutional order will excessively diminish government support for the crucial role of religious piety.

**C.** They point to the proposed constitution's silence on God's supreme authority, in contrast with the existing Articles of Confederation, which close with an acknowledgment of the ultimate political rule of God.

**D.** Some Anti-Federalists are troubled by the proposed constitution's outlawing of any religious test for holding office.

**E.** The Anti-Federalists see state governments as better suited to provide government support for local Protestant sects. These state establishments of religion are understood to go along with what the Maryland Anti-Federalist John Mercer terms local "laws of morality."

**III.** Anti-Federalists argue that, at the state and local levels, government is smaller in scale and hence less domineering.

- **A.** Government at the state and local levels tends to involve more people, thus keeping control in the people's hands and guarding against aristocratic tendencies.
  - **1.** This popular participation in government is most widely activated through service on civil and criminal juries.
  - **2.** The Anti-Federalists warn that the proposed constitution will contribute to a weakening of the people's democratic control over the judicial branch of government by instituting a diminution of the power of popular juries.

- **B.** Juries at the time of the founding sometimes had not only the right and power to determine matters of fact but also the right and power to interpret the meaning of the law.
  - **1.** This was a right and power rooted not only in classical republicanism but also in the English tradition celebrated by Montesquieu.
  - **2.** It was this power in the juries that made them key democratic checks on aristocratic judicial activism.

- **C.** Anti-Federalists correctly foresee and warn that under the proposed constitution, juries will lose the right to interpret the meaning of the law.
  - **1.** Juries will be limited to judging only the facts of the case before them.

2. Regarding the power of interpreting the law, the Anti-Federalists warn that this power will be handed over entirely to the unelected judges, who will thus become a kind of aristocracy.

3. The Anti-Federalists see that the aristocratic federal courts are given the right, under the proposed constitution, to overturn local democratic jury verdicts.

IV. The Anti-Federalists argue that the legislative branch of government should be kept under local, popular control as well.

A. The Anti-Federalists argue that, at the state level, elected representatives are more truly representative and responsive to the people's will for three reasons.

1. The state legislators meet at a place closer to the people and are thus better observed by the people.

2. The state legislators tend to live more among the people and as a result are better known to the people.

3. The state legislators tend to resemble or mirror the people's own character.

B. The Anti-Federalists add that it is only such representatives, whom the people know as kindred spirits, that the people will readily obey and follow with trust.

C. The Anti-Federalists also argue that if the power is kept more at the state and local levels, then there is more likelihood of the elected representatives coming from the agrarian middle class of yeomen (small farmers who own their own land) who cannot easily afford to stand for office but who are more likely to do so if the seat of government is closer.

1. Having representatives who are yeomen tends to keep leaders and the populace more moderate in their love of wealth, making the leadership less tempted by greed and ambition and the populace less likely to divide into hostile classes.

2. This preserves more of the classical homogeneity of lifestyle needed for a communal spirit.

3. The leadership of yeoman farmers at the state and local levels will tend to instill in society the healthy influence of people who are economically self-sufficient and thus independent in spirit.

**V.** It is time to consider the arguments and grounds upon which *The Federalist* takes its stand in response to these ideas.

    **A.** The rhetorical strategy of the papers is not one of defense but of offense.

    **B.** They launch their counterattack by spotlighting the necessities of national defense and foreign policy.

        **1.** John Jay points out that in order not to give other nations just causes for conflict with America, the country must faithfully observe international law and custom; such fidelity is more likely with a unified government that can authoritatively control all foreign relations.

        **2.** In the absence of a centralized government, the different states are too likely to be tempted to vary in the way they interpret and abide by national obligations and are too likely to drag the rest of the nation into wars over local quarrels.

        **3.** Jay argues that a strong central government will tend to draw leaders who are more prudent regarding foreign affairs.

        **4.** Jay argues that a strong central government will deter foreign powers from being tempted to take advantage of the weakness of a looser confederacy.

        **5.** Jay and Hamilton argue that to effectively deter European commercial empires from dominating and intimidating us, we must put power in the central government to raise and maintain unified naval and land forces.

        **6.** This military power must include the ability to organize, regulate, and employ the state militias, as well as the authority for a standing army and navy during peacetime.

    **C.** Hamilton makes clear that the central government cannot have these powers without the unlimited power of taxation, necessary to raise the revenues upon which these military powers depend.

    **D.** The opening argument by Jay and Hamilton already elaborated a standard by which to judge the adequacy of the powers of any government for America.

        **1.** By this standard, Hamilton proceeds to judge as grossly inadequate the existing Articles of Confederation.

        **2.** Hamilton and Madison go on to argue that, on the basis of the needs of national security, there is a decisive inadequacy in any and all confederate systems throughout history.

**Essential Reading:**

"Brutus" [probably Robert Yates], First Essay; in Storing, *The Complete Anti-Federalist*, Vol. 2, pp. 363–72.

"The Federal Farmer" [probably Richard Henry Lee], Second Letter; in Storing, *The Complete Anti-Federalist*, Vol. 2, pp. 230–34.

*The Federalist*, Papers 2–5, 11, and 12.

Jefferson, *Notes on the State of Virginia*, Query 17, *The Founders' Constitution*, Chapter 4, Number 9.

Smith, speeches at the New York Ratifying Convention (June 21, 1788); in Storing, *The Complete Anti-Federalist*, Vol. 6, pp. 155–61.

**Supplementary Reading:**

Storing, *What the Anti-Federalists Were For*, Chapter 3.

**Questions to Consider:**

1. What are the key reasons why the Anti-Federalists think governmental power should be weighted more in favor of state and local government? How persuasive do you find these reasons?

2. What exactly is the tension in the Anti-Federalist republican vision between the classical civic ideal and the independent yeoman farmer ideal? Do you think this tension can be lived with, or is it likely to lead to unmanageable problems in practice?

# Lecture Three—Transcript
## The Anti-Federalists' Republican Vision

In the last lecture, we saw how the Anti-Federalists make a qualified but still strong appeal to the classical republican heritage, qualified because the Anti-Federalists are by no means simply classical republicans. They share with the Federalists and with Americans generally, a republican vision that is much less communal, much more individualistic and commercial, than the classical ideal. Their highest priority, shared with the Federalists, is the protection of individual rights and liberties.

But the Anti-Federalists contend that, precisely in order to protect those individualist rights and liberties, substantial ingredients of the old classical ideal in its Montesquieuan democratic reformulation remain essential. As the Pennsylvania writer who calls himself "A Federal Republican" puts it, "Whatever the refinement of modern politics may inculcate, it still is certain that some degree of virtue must exist, or freedom cannot live."

The Anti-Federalist position is vividly illustrated by what they say as regards religion. Anti-Federalists as well as Federalists are committed to individual religious freedom and hence, religious diversity. Yet, at the same time, the Anti-Federalists, like most Americans of the time, assume that the religious diversity would and should be a Christian and even a mainly Protestant diversity. What's more, they are convinced that Protestant Christian piety and religious education, in the populace, are essential foundations for civic virtue, and citizenship education. Without widespread belief in a God who stands behind law-abiding justice, sanctioning morality with rewards and punishments in a life to come, too many people are tempted, they think, to neglect their demanding civic duties for the sake of pursuing their selfish material interests.

In the Constitutional Convention itself, Benjamin Franklin, in a major speech on June 28, had pleaded, unsuccessfully, for the convention to return to the prayerful piety that had helped inspire the Revolution.

> I have lived, [Franklin declared] a long time, and the longer I live, the more convincing proofs I see of this truth, that God governs in the affairs of men. ... We have been assured, Sir, in the sacred writings that, "except the Lord build the House, they labor in vain that build it," I firmly believe this, [Franklin says.]

> And I also believe that without his concurring aid we shall succeed in this political building no better than the builders of Babel. We

shall be divided by our little partial local interests. Our projects will be confounded, and we ourselves shall become a reproach and by ward down to future ages. And what is worse, mankind may hereafter from this unfortunate instance, despair of establishing Governments by Human Wisdom, and leave it to chance, war and conquest.

Now the Anti-Federalists share Franklin's deep worry. They warn that the proposed constitutional order will excessively diminish governmental support for this crucial role of Christian piety and religiously-based virtue in civic life and education. The Anti-Federalists point with dismay to the proposed constitution's stony silence on God and God's supreme authority, which is in striking contrast to the existing constitution, The Articles of Confederation, which close with an acknowledgement of the ultimate political rule of God.

Some of the Anti-Federalists are troubled by the proposed constitution's outlawing of any religious test for holding office, in Article VI, Section 3 of the Constitution. Thus, an Anti-Federalist writer who significantly signs himself with the biblical pen name "Samuel" protests that the President and Congress "may consist," he says, "of men of no principle, for no religion is required, as any qualification, to fill any and every seat."

Moreover, one major reason why the Anti-Federalists argue that more power should be left to the states and localities is that they see state governments are better suited to provide government support, through tax dollars, for local Protestant sects. The sort of limited establishment of religion, rooted in local community sentiment, that already existed, at that time in many of the states and that continue to exist well into the 19th century.

These state establishments of religion were understood to go along with what the Maryland Anti-Federalist John Mercer terms local "laws of morality," laws that, as he puts it, "would prohibit the abuse of wealth," and institute a "council of censors, to punish offenders. On the model," he says, "of the small Swiss federal republics, above all Calvinist Geneva."

But the concern for government support for religion and religiously-based moral education is only one part of the reasons why the Anti-Federalists argue that the needed ingredients of the classical ideal will be better maintained by keeping the balance of power weighted more toward state and local government.

Even more important, they argue, is the fact that, at the state and local level, government is smaller in scale, hence less overbearing and domineering. By the same token, and still more important, government at the state and local level tends to involve the people more, to demand more from the people, thus keeping control in the people's hands, preventing and guarding against elite, aristocratic tendencies. This popular participation in and thus control over the government is most widely activated through what Richard Henry Lee calls the people's "just and rightful control in the judicial," branch, that is, through their service on civil and criminal juries.

The Anti-Federalists warn that this proposed constitution is going to contribute to a grave weakening of the people's democratic control over the judicial branch of the government, by instituting a drastic diminution of the power of popular juries in America, which will mutilate, they say, what is perhaps the most important institution for participatory democracy.

Now to understand what the Anti-Federalists are getting at, in this warning, we must bear in mind an important historical fact about what the power of juries was in America at that time. Juries at the time of the founding had not only the right and power to determine matters of fact in the case before them, but also the right and power to interpret the meaning of the law. This was a right and power rooted in classical republicanism, but not only there, but also in English tradition, celebrated by Montesquieu, who interpreted the British constitution as placing the judicial branch in the hands of the people, through the supreme power of the popular juries. It was above all this power in the juries, to participate in interpreting the law and even to overrule judges' interpretations of the law that made juries key democratic checks on aristocratic judicial activism. Anti-Federalists like "The Federal Farmer" correctly predicted and foresaw that under the proposed constitution, juries will lose the right to interpret the meaning of the law. Juries will be limited, they said, and they were right, to judging only the facts of the case before them. As regards to the more important power, to interpret the law, the Anti-Federalists correctly warn this basic, traditionally democratic power will be entirely handed over to the unelected judges, who will thus become a kind of aristocracy, dominating the judicial branch.

As John Mercer puts it, the jury, he says, "is the democratic branch of the judiciary power," and as such is even "more necessary than representatives in the legislature. Why," Mercer asks, "shall we risk this important check to judiciary usurpation, provided by the wisdom of antiquity? It's by the attacks on private property, through the judiciary, that despotism becomes as irresistible as terrible," he writes.

In addition, making things even worse in their view, the Anti-Federalists see that these aristocratic federal courts are given under this constitution the right to overturn local democratic jury verdicts, meaning to say, that jury verdicts will no longer be final. The Anti-Federalists point out that by Article 3, Section 2, clause 2, of the proposed constitution, the Supreme Court is given "appellate Jurisdiction, both as to law and fact."

It's of course not only the judicial branch of government that the Anti-Federalists see as best kept under local, popular control. Equally important, they argue, is keeping the legislative branch under such control as much as possible. The Anti-Federalists argue that at the state level, elected representatives are more truly representative and responsive to the people's will, and for three major reasons they argue. First, the state legislators meet at a place, the state capitol that is closer to the people and thus better observed by the people. Second, the state legislators tend to live more among the people and as a result are better known to the people, in their personal lives and their character. Third, the state legislators tend to resemble or mirror better the people's own character. They tend less to be an elite that lives a lifestyle unlike that of the people.

Here the Anti-Federalists, in effect, articulate a specific theory of what genuinely democratic representation ought to mean. Melancton Smith, the leading Anti-Federalist speaker and debate opponent of Hamilton in the New York Convention puts it this way, "The idea that naturally suggests itself to our minds, when we speak of representatives is, that they resemble those they represent; they should be a true picture of the people ... [and] sympathize in all their distresses." Or in the words of Samuel Chase, who had been a leader of the Revolution in Maryland, "A representative should be the image of those he represents. He should know their sentiments and their wants and their desires—he should possess their feelings—he should be governed by their interests with which his own should be inseparably connected." The Anti-Federalists add, it's only such representatives, whom the people truly know as kindred spirits, that the people will readily obey and follow with trust.

As "Brutus" says, "The confidence which the people have in their rulers, in a free republic, arises from their knowing them." No one expressed the critical bite of the Anti-Federalist theory of representation better than an unknown Massachusetts writer who signed himself "Cornelius." He put it this way:

> The members of our State legislature, [he pointed out,] are annually elected. They are subject to instructions. They are chosen within small circles. They are sent but a small distance from their respective homes. They frequently see and are seen, by the men whose servants they are. They return and mix with their neighbors of the lowest rank, see their poverty, and feel their wants. On the contrary, the members of the proposed Congress are to be chosen for a term of years. They are to be subject to no instructions. They are to be chosen within large circles. They'll be unknown to a considerable part of their constituents and their constituents will be not less unknown to them. They will be far removed and long detained, from the view of their constituents. Their general conduct will be unknown. Their chief connections will be with men of the first rank in the United States, who have been bred in affluence at least, if not in the excess of luxury. Let anyone judge, whether they will long retain the same ideas as their constituents.

Finally, the Anti-Federalists also argue that if the power is kept more at the state and local level, then there is more likelihood of the elected representatives coming from the agrarian middle class farmers, yeoman, as they put it, or small farmers who own their own land, who can not easily afford to stand for office, if they have to travel far away from their farms to serve for long periods, in some distant national capital, but who are more likely to be able to serve if the seat of government is closer by, and the meetings shorter or frequently interrupted. Having representatives who are yeomen tends to keep leaders, as well as the populace less luxurious, more moderate in their love of money and in their wealth, making the leadership less tempted to luxurious greed and ambition and making the populace less likely to divide into hostile classes separated by vast disparities of wealth and economic interest, thus preserving more of the classical homogeneity and similarity of lifestyle that's needed for fraternal and communal spirit.

Where, as the writer who signs himself "Cato" says, in his third letter, "Acquaintance, habits, and fortunes, nourish affection, and attachment." Or as "Brutus" says, in his first essay, "In a republic, the manners, sentiments, and interests of the people should be similar. If this be not the case, there'll be a constant clashing of opinions. And the representatives of one part will be continually striving against those of another."

Echoing a major thesis of Aristotle's *Politics*, Melancton Smith, in debating Alexander Hamilton in the New York Ratifying Convention said:

Those in middling circumstances have less temptation. They're inclined by habit and the company with whom they associate, to set bounds to their passions and appetites. If this is not sufficient, the want of means to gratify them will be a restraint. They're obliged to employ their time in their respective callings, hence the substantial yeomanry of the country are more temperate, of better morals and less ambition than the great. The latter do not feel for the poor and middling class. A representative body, composed principally of respectable yeomanry, is the best possible security to liberty. The interest of both the rich and the poor are involved in that of the middling class. No burden can be laid on the poor, but what will sensibly affect the middling class. And any law rendering property insecure would be injurious to the rich. When therefore this yeoman class in society, pursue their own interest, they promote that of the public, for it is involved in it.

In addition to promoting moderate wealth, and similarity and fellow-feeling, the leadership of yeoman farmers at the state and local level will bring yet another great civic good, the Anti-Federalists argue. It will tend to instill throughout society the healthy influence of people who are more economically self-sufficient, and thus more independent in spirit. No one expressed this thought more eloquently than Thomas Jefferson, who characterized himself, in a famous letter as, "Neither Federalist nor Anti-federalist." Who, in other words, saw himself as straddling the Great Debate and seeing wisdom in both sides. Jefferson's most important, and somewhat classical sounding pronouncement on the moral superiority of putting power in local government dominated by the small farmers is found in the one book he ever published, *Notes on the State of Virginia*, which was published in the same year as *The Federalist*, and during the constitutional debates.

There Jefferson says, in a famous passage:

Those who labor in the earth are the chosen people of God, if ever he had a chosen people, whose breasts he has made the peculiar deposit for substantial and genuine virtue. It is the focus in which he keeps alive that sacred fire, which otherwise might escape from the face of the earth. Corruption of morals in the mass of cultivators is a phenomenon of which no age, nor nation, has furnished an example. It is the mark set on those, who not looking up to heaven, to their own soil and industry, as does the husbandman,

… which is a term, a term he uses for the farmer, for their subsistence, depend for it on the casualties and caprice of customers.

> Dependence begets subservience and venality, suffocates the germ of virtue, and prepares fit tools for the designs of ambition. This, the natural progress and consequence of the arts has sometimes perhaps been retarded by accidental circumstances, but generally speaking, the proportion which the aggregate of the other classes of citizens bears in any state to that of its husbandmen is the proportion of its unsound to its healthy parts, and is a good enough barometer whereby to measure its degree of corruption. While we have land to labor then, let us never wish to see our citizens occupied at a work bench. Let our workshops remain in Europe. It is better to carry provisions and materials to workman there then bring them to the provisions and materials and with them their manners and principles. The loss by the transportation of commodities across the Atlantic will be made up in happiness and permanence of government. The mobs of great cities add just so much to the support of pure government as sores do to the strength of the human body. It is the manners and spirit of a people, which preserve a republican figure, a degeneracy in these is a canker, which soon eats to the heart of its laws and Constitution. Corruption of morals in the mass of farmers is a phenomenon of which no age nor nation has furnished an example. It is the mark set on those who not looking up to heaven to their own soil and industry, as does the farmer for their subsistence, depend for it on the casualties and caprice of customers. Dependence begets subservience and venality, suffocates the germ of virtue and prepares fit tools for the designs of ambition. Generally speaking, the proportion which the aggregate of the other classes of citizens bears in any state to that of its husbandmen or farmers is the proportion of the unsound to its healthy parts.

Now at this point, with the Anti-Federalist critique laid out, it's time for us to turn to consider the arguments and grounds upon which *The Federalist Papers* take their stand in response.

To begin with, what we see as we open *The Federalist* and read on through the first few papers is that their rhetorical strategy is not one of defense, but rather of offense, or counter-attack on a new flank. They launch their counter-attack by an initial shift of focus, change of subject. *The Federalist Papers* began not by taking up and responding to the challenge laid down by the Anti-Federalists as to how republican liberty is to be maintained in domestic civil life. Instead, "Publius" switches the subject to national security, switches the spotlight to the necessities of national defense and foreign policy and argues that these are the necessities that most obviously require a much more consolidated and powerful central government. If we look at the actual text of the Constitution itself and we see that of the 18 enumerated powers given to the national legislature, in Article 1, Section 8, fully only half of those pertain to defense and foreign affairs.

The argument on this basis of national security starts with John Jay pointing out, in the third paper, that in order not to give other nations plausibly just causes for conflict with America, the country as a whole, and all its citizens, must faithfully observe international law and custom and especially all sworn treaty obligations and such fidelity is much more likely, he argues, with a unified, central government that can authoritatively and reliably control all foreign relations and exercise its authority directly on individual citizens, as well as on state and local governments. Doing so, not only, he argues, through a powerful legislature and executive, but also through a national judiciary whose interpretations of law, in relation to foreigners, are final and binding on everyone.

In the absence of such a strong centralized government, Jay argues, the different states, and the individuals in each state, are all too likely as is happening right now, Jay says, to be tempted, by their immediate and local interests, to vary widely and provocatively in the way they interpret and abide by international obligations, and are all too likely to drag the whole rest of the nation into wars over what are essentially local quarrels inflamed by local passions in regard to Indian tribes as well as bordering European empires.

Besides, Jay argues, a strong central government will tend to draw to it leaders who are more prudent than far-sighted as regards foreign affairs, leaders who will, by the great responsibilities of their national offices, tend to have a broader and less parochial regard for the overall interests of the whole country and in addition, will be able to negotiate with foreign powers from a position of greater strength and hence advantage.

What's more, Jay goes on to argue in the fourth paper, a strong central government will deter foreign powers from being tempted to take advantage of the weakness, disunity, and fractiousness of a looser confederacy. There will be plenty of occasions for such temptations, Jay warns, and later

Hamilton warns about this danger of fractiousness even more emphatically, especially in Papers 11 and 24.

America's seafaring commerce already, Hamilton says, excites great rivalry from European commercial powers, who would like, Hamilton says in his words, to "clip the wings on which we might soar to a dangerous greatness." European manufacturing powers will want access to and if possible dominance over the growing consumer market within America, Hamilton warns, and the Spanish and British empires surround America and dominate the West Indies.

Jay and Hamilton argue, if we are going to effectively deter these great European commercial empires from exercising domination through intimidation over us, then we must put power in the central government to raise and maintain unified naval and land forces, of whatever size may be judged necessary. This military power in the central government must include the ability to organize and regulate and employ the state militias and, as Jay puts it, "in a manner consolidate them into one corps" referring to Article 1, Section 8, Clause 16 of the Constitution which indicates just that. But this power must also include, Jay argues, the authority to maintain a standing, professional national army, as well as a navy, in peacetime.

As Hamilton makes much clearer in the subsequent Papers 12 and later, especially Papers 30 through 36, the central government cannot have these powers, without having also, what he calls, the unlimited power of taxation, which is necessary to raise the revenues upon which a powerful military defense can be built. We notice that the very first of the enumerated powers given to the national legislature under Article 1, Section 8 of the Constitution is the taxation power. The Constitution views the taxation power as the primary power of government.

In this opening argument, Jay and Hamilton have, in effect, elaborated the standard set by the exigencies of foreign affairs and national security, by which, they contend, one must judge the adequacy of the powers of any government for America. By this standard, Hamilton proceeds, in the papers starting with number 15, to judge as grossly inadequate the existing Articles of Confederation. More importantly and more generally, he and then Madison go on to argue, that on this basis, on the basis of the needs of national security, there is a decisive inadequacy in any and all confederate systems, throughout all past history. All confederacies, such as are envisioned as ideal by the Anti-Federalists, they argue, have been disasters from the point of view of national security and foreign and defense policy.

In the next lecture we'll follow the elaboration of this critique of confederation, on the basis primarily of the needs of national security and then we'll look to see how the Anti-Federalists respond, or what is their conception of the needs of foreign policy and defense.

# Lecture Four
# The Argument over National Security

**Scope:**  On the grounds of what is needed for sound defense and foreign policy, "Publius" articulates a critique of the Articles of Confederation and then moves to a more general critique of the inadequacy of confederacies. This analysis teaches, "Publius" argues, that what American national security requires is a central government that has "unlimited" military and taxation powers that can be applied to individual citizens directly and not merely through their state governments. The Anti-Federalists respond by contending that such "unlimited" powers in the central government are unnecessary for national security and dangerous to liberty. These powers should be limited by being shared with the state governments. Reliance should be placed not on a professional army, but rather on state-based citizen militias, in accord with the classical republican tradition. The Anti-Federalists voice the suspicion that the Federalists, in their stress on foreign and military policy, are not merely thinking of defense but are in some measure falling prey to the enchantment of visions of national glory and empire.

## Outline

I. Whereas the Anti-Federalist attack focuses on the dangers that the proposed constitutional system poses to republican freedom in domestic life, the Federalist response begins not with a defense but with a counterattack on a different front.

    **A.** *The Federalist* starts off by shifting the spotlight to the necessities of national security.

    **B.** Even though they stress foreign and defense policy, Hamilton and Madison do not neglect domestic policy, but these concerns are treated as continuous with concerns of foreign policy.

II. It is on this ground of foreign and defense policy that *The Federalist* critiques the total inadequacy of the existing system under the Articles of Confederation. "Publius" sums up the worst features of the contemporary state of the United States in *Federalist* 15 and subsequent papers, especially *Federalist* 22 and 24.

A. To appreciate all that "Publius" is referring to, we need to flesh out what is going on in foreign affairs in 1787.
   1. The United States is in violation of its obligations to England under the peace treaty that ended the Revolutionary War, especially its obligations to return or pay for property taken from loyalists during the war.
   2. Despite treaties with Spain, Americans are forbidden access to the entire Mississippi River; Spain maintains forts and Indian allies who control much of the territory of Alabama, Mississippi, Tennessee, and Kentucky.
   3. The United States can raise no adequate armed forces to defend these borders and have no adequate defense on the seas and coasts, which leaves American shipping unprotected.
   4. The United States is unable to pay its debts incurred during the American Revolution.
   5. The result of this is that no foreign country will consider entering into negotiations to make additional treaties for the sake of commerce and security.
B. Hamilton and Madison argue that this recent American experience is an illustration of the weakness within all confederations.
   1. At the core of all the failures of confederacies throughout history is the predominance of the principle that the central government cannot legislate for individual citizens directly but only indirectly, through legislating for state governments.
   2. History shows that the predominance of this principle leads to one of two outcomes: the "natural death" or the "violent death" of the confederacy.
   3. By "natural death," "Publius" means that the confederacy sooner or later dissolves because the central government cannot enforce its own laws. The "violent death" of confederacies occurs when the central government finally resorts to armed force and creates a standing army with which to intimidate the state governments into compliance.
   4. Confederacies have been able to escape these two fates only to the degree to which they have learned the need for a strong central government to which they give the power to command and tax individuals directly.
C. The full reach of this argument becomes clear only when we put it together with what "Publius" argues concerning the precise extent

of the power that has to be given to the central government to allow it to meet the requirements of foreign policy and defense.

    **1.** The powers that the central government must be given in order to carry out its responsibility for defense have to be unlimited.

    **2.** Hamilton makes explicit in Papers 30 and 31 that this means the central government must have what he calls "an unrestrained power of taxation."

**III.** One finds among Anti-Federalists a deep tendency to discount the gravity of the dangers posed by foreign policy and defense, at least for the American situation in the foreseeable future.

    **A.** The Anti-Federalists stress America's isolated position, separated by oceans from the European powers.

    **B.** The Anti-Federalists argue that when defensive warfare is required, healthy republics can and should put their trust in the fighting spirit of the civilian populace—organized in state militias.

        **1.** Militias should, in peacetime, remain solely managed by the states.

        **2.** "The Federal Farmer" does not deny the need for some regular or professional troops on guard duty, but he warns of the dangerous power given to the federal government under the proposed constitution's article of establishing a full-scale standing army in peacetime, which the Anti-Federalists decry as the basis for a separate military establishment opposed to the interest of the civilian population.

    **C.** Power over "the purse and the sword" should be lodged with the state and local governments.

        **1.** It is too dangerous and unnecessary to bestow permanent unlimited military and taxation powers on the central government; instead, in the event of emergencies these powers can be granted temporarily to the central government.

        **2.** Such grants should be made only in the face of threats that are recognized and agreed on by the vast majority of the people through their state governments.

    **D.** Anti-Federalists argue it is too dangerous to design the powers of the central government for the sake of possible emergencies.

        **1.** They stress that it is a universal experience that governments always tend to maximize whatever taxation and spending powers are given to them.

**2.** It is therefore safest to give to government at the start the least power possible.

**E.** This kind of thinking spurs the suspicion repeatedly voiced by the Anti-Federalists that the Federalists, in their stress on the extraordinary demands of foreign and defense policy, are falling prey to the enchantment of visions of national greatness, which is a temptation that will sound the death knell of small-scale republican freedom and virtue.

## Essential Reading:

"Brutus," Eighth Essay; in Storing, *The Complete Anti-Federalist*, Vol. 2, pp. 405–7.

"The Federal Farmer," first seven paragraphs of 18th Letter; in Storing, *The Complete Anti-Federalist*, Vol. 2, pp. 339–43.

*The Federalist*, Papers 15–36 and 41 (review Papers 2–4).

## Supplementary Reading:

Marks, *Independence on Trial*, Chapters 1 and 4.

## Questions to Consider:

**1.** What are the strengths and weaknesses in the Federalists' argument that national security requires that "unlimited" military and taxation powers be granted to the central government? Are you convinced by their argument? Why or why not?

**2.** What do the differing strategies and choices of focus, in their respective arguments, reveal about the different priorities of the Federalists and Anti-Federalists?

# Lecture Four—Transcript
## The Argument over National Security

At the end of the last lecture, we began to see the initial strategy and substance of the Federalist reply to the Anti-Federalist attack. Whereas the Anti-Federalist's attack focusing on the dangers that the proposed constitutional system poses to republican freedom in domestic civic life, the Federalist response begins, not with a defense responding to this attack but instead by launching a counter-attack, on a different front.

*The Federalist Papers* start off by shifting the spotlight chiefly to the necessities of national security. This choice of emphasis on the exigencies of foreign more than on those of domestic policy continues through the first half of *The Federalist Papers,* the part of the papers that's devoted to the general, overall, thematic argument for the new constitution. Now to be sure, even though they stress foreign and defense policy, Hamilton and Madison do not neglect domestic or internal policy. "Publius" treats as very important the regulation and facilitation of interstate commerce and the maintenance of domestic peace and security. But even these major domestic concerns are treated as continuous with, if not subordinate to, the concerns of foreign policy. This is made especially clear in the two authoritative brief statements of the main purposes of the proposed constitutional union. One is given by Hamilton at the start of Paper 23 and the other is given by Madison near the beginning of Paper 41. If one examines each of those passages, one sees that they list the purposes of the new constitution in such a way as to make it clear that the chief purposes revolve around national security and foreign affairs.

It is on this ground, of foreign and defense policy, primarily, that *The Federalist Papers* proceed to elaborate, in Papers 15 and following, a critique of the total inadequacy, in their view, of the existing constitutional system, under the Articles of Confederation. Then "Publius" moves, on the basis of this critique of the existing constitution, to a more general critique of federalism or confederacies altogether chiefly on grounds of national security.

"Publius" sums up the worst features of the contemporary state of things under the Articles of Confederation in the 15th *Federalist* paper. It's a summary which he elaborates in previous as well as subsequent papers and especially in Papers 22 and 24. To appreciate fully all that "Publius" is referring to, we need to flesh out his allusions to what is actually going on in foreign affairs at this time in 1787.

First and foremost, the United States are in violation of their obligations to England under the peace treaty that ended the Revolutionary War, especially obligations to return or to pay for property taken from loyalists during the war. During the Revolution thousands of loyalists lost their property in confiscations of all kinds. It was a solemn promise in the treaty that ended the Revolution that that property would be restored or paid for by the Americans, and the existing Congress is simply unable to compel the states and the individuals in the states to abide by or fulfill these solemn obligations. This is giving the British an excuse and more than an excuse, a justification, for not upholding their end of the treaty. The British have refused to abandon their forts in U.S. territory, forts which stretch a thousand miles from Lake Champlain to Lake Superior. The British are also refusing to disband thousands of Tories who are in armed camps on the northern borders. Worst of all, the British are supporting large, hostile Indian tribes like the Iroquois; and they're doing all this with the perfect justification excuse of saying, look, we aren't going to disband the armed camps of Tories until you give the Tories back what you promised to give them.

Meanwhile, in the South and West, despite treaties with Spain—that European power continues—in violation of treaties, to forbid Americans access to the entire Mississippi River, and still worse, to maintain forts and Indian allies, that in effect control much of the territory of Alabama, Mississippi, Tennessee, Kentucky—the United States, "Publius" points out, can raise no adequate armed forces to defend any of these borders: North, South, or West. The entire national armed forces consist of 700 men, many of them without boots or ammunition, even though Congress has voted to raise and equip a large army, but Congress cannot get the states to give the money to do so.

For defense on the seas and the coasts, Hamilton points out, there's no national navy whatsoever. America doesn't have a single ship which leaves shipping completely unprotected. Our shipping is at present, Hamilton points out, prey to barbary pirates and with a great naval war looming in Europe between France and England, this leaves American shipping vulnerable to all sorts of hostile pressures from both sides in this inevitably coming war.

In addition to all this, "Publius" stresses, the United States is totally unable to pay its debts incurred during the Revolution. Both foreign and domestic creditors and bond holders are just not being paid and hence the nation has no credit and hence can't borrow a dime for all kinds of needed funds and projects. The result of all this taken together, "Publius" points out, is that no foreign country will even consider entering into negotiations with this new

United States, to make all sorts of needed additional treaties for the sake of commerce and security. Our credit is at nil, Hamilton says, and our credibility is also at nil.

Hamilton and Madison then proceed to argue that these gross failings are not the result of some incidental or secondary mistakes in the design of the system that can be somehow remedied by amendments that will make a better Confederacy or a better Confederation. No, they contend, this recent American experience is only a vivid, present illustration of the grave general weaknesses with all confederations. The fundamental weakness of Confederation, as Hamilton puts it at the start of Paper 16 is "... equally attested by the events which have befallen all other governments of the confederate kind." Hamilton and Madison support this by an analysis in Papers 16 through 20 of the entire recorded history of confederacies, stretching from ancient Greece to the contemporary Netherlands, and they tried to show that at the core of all the failures of confederacies throughout history is what Hamilton calls their "great and radical vice," which is, the predominance of this principle, that the federal or central government cannot legislate for or exercise command over or raise taxes from, the individual citizens directly but can only act on and command and seek revenue from, the member state governments, which latter alone have the right to act on and rule directly the individual citizens. That's the principle of a Confederation, and that principle is destructive, Hamilton says.

Hamilton argues that the predominance of this pernicious principle, inevitably leads to one of two disastrous outcomes. What Hamilton calls, either the natural death of the Confederacy or, as he puts it, the violent death of the Confederacy. That's what's going to happen to us and is already happening, he says. Now, by the natural death, he means, the Confederacy sooner or later dissolves and that results because the central government cannot enforce its laws and commands and judicial decisions. So, as Hamilton puts it, these laws become mere recommendations to the state governments, dependent for their effect on the voluntary acquiesce of each state one by one, with a result that they're more and more ignored. This naturally happens, Hamilton says, on account of two things. First, what he calls the proud and selfish love of power that tends to inspirit each independent state government, and also on account of the reluctance each state has, even if it has good intentions to be the first to make the sacrifices of its own narrow interests for the good of the whole.

Now, the other alternative outcome, Hamilton says, is what he calls the violent death of Confederacies, and that occurs where the central government finally decides that it's got to resort to armed force to compel the states and creates some kind of confederal police force or standing army that is independent of the states, with which to control or intimidate the member state governments into compliance. The consequence of that is civil war, endless civil strife between the state militias and the central military, leading eventually to somebody's despotism. Either a despotism exercised by the central government, with some kind of dominating elite military power, or a despotism of a central government that has actually become the tool of one or more of the biggest and most powerful states who have won out in the fratricidal struggle or as the tool of some great outside power, which has been invited to intervene by some of the weaker losing states in the fratricidal struggle.

If you look at the history of Confederacy, "Publius" argues, you will find no other alternatives than these that we have just laid out. Confederacies have been able to postpone one of these fates only to the degree to which they've learned this lesson; and that is the need to create a strong central government to which they give the power to command and tax individual citizens directly and not have to go through the state governments.

The full reach and radicalism of this argument becomes clear only when we put it together with what "Publius" is arguing concerning the precise extent of this power that has to be given to the central government over individuals to allow it to meet the needs of foreign policy and national security especially. Because in this context, "Publius" makes no bones about declaring that the powers that the central government must be given in order to carry out its national security responsibilities have to be unlimited, without any limit.

> These powers, [he declares in Paper 23] ought to exist without limitation, because it is impossible to foresee or to define the extent and variety of national exigencies, and the correspondent extent and variety of the means which may be necessary to satisfy them. The circumstances that endanger the safety of nations are infinite and for this reason, no constitutional shackles can wisely be imposed on the power to which the care of it is committed. There can be no limitation," he says, "of that authority, which is to provide for the defense and protection of the community, in any matter essential to its efficacy.

The Founders "Publius" and Madison make it very clear, make no mistake, they say, we are creating under this constitution a government, which will have unlimited authority to do whatever it thinks necessary for national security. There is no constitutional limitation on that.

To make the economic point very clear, Hamilton subsequently makes explicit, in Papers 30 and 31, that this means the central government must have, what he calls, "an unrestrained power of taxation" over every individual. In other words, the central government must have the power to tax people to the hilt, if necessary. Hamilton acknowledges that, as he puts it, "The antagonists of the proposed constitution" seem "to make their principal and most zealous effort against this part of the plan." That is certainly true. Thus the Anti-Federalist who signs himself "Brutus" says, in his eighth essay, "These powers taken in connection, amount to this, that the general government have unlimited authority and control over all the wealth and all the force of the union. What kind of freedom or independency is left to the state governments, when they cannot command any part of the property or the force of the country, but at the will of Congress?"

In response, Hamilton insists on what he calls the sheer, "irresistible," as he puts it, logic of the proposition, that, as he puts it in Paper 31, "There ought to be no limitation of a power destined to effect a purpose which is itself incapable of limitation." Or as Madison later, in Paper 41, explains:

> If a federal Constitution could chain the ambition or set bounds to the exertions of all other nations, then indeed might it prudently chain the discretion of its own government and set bounds to the exertions of its own safety.

But that's a foolish dream, Madison says, you have to be totally irresponsible to think that in foreign policy you can put limits on what your government can and should do to provide for national security when you face, as they've said earlier, the infinity of evil enemies can do. So it's simply impossible to think that way, Madison says, and, therefore, it was "necessary," he continues, "to give an indefinite power of raising troops, as well as providing fleets and of maintaining both in peace as well as in war."

So this is another crucial factor that is driven home by Hamilton and Madison. We're not just talking about war time, they say, in peace time, too, the federal government under this constitution is being given the authority to do anything it wants and needs to do in its judgment that is necessary for national security.

Both Hamilton and Madison stress in this context that, as Hamilton says in Paper 34, "We must bear in mind, that we are not to confine our view to the present period, but to look forward to remote futurity … the probable exigencies of ages …" and in this light, Hamilton says, "the exigencies of the union could be susceptible of no limits, even in the imagination." That's how strong he goes. "You can't imagine," he says, "what the limits are that we're giving to the government. There are no imagined limits because there are no imagined limits to the threats we may have to face."

What kind of a response do the Anti-Federalist writings make to this whole line of remarkable argument, concerning the unlimited requirements of national security and foreign and defense policy? Well, to begin with, one finds among the Anti-Federalists a deep tendency to discount the gravity of the dangers posed by and therefore the degree of importance that the Federalists give to national security, foreign policy, defense, at least for the American situation in the foreseeable future. This is an important difference between the Federalist and the Anti-Federalist. Typically, the Anti-Federalist will argue, "Well, in the foreseeable future, why should we need a large navy and standing army?" Hamilton, as we've just seen in the quote I read, of course comes back saying we have to think for a long future and who knows what this nation is going to have to face.

But the "The Federal Farmer," for example, in his first letter, says, "We're in a state of perfect peace and in no danger of any invasions. The state governments are in the full exercise of their powers. And our governments answer all present exigencies." Similarly, Patrick Henry proclaims, "On a fair investigation, we shall be found to be surrounded by no real dangers. Our political and natural hemisphere are now equally tranquil."

The Anti-Federalists typically stress America's isolated position, separated by oceans from the European powers. Thus "Brutus" says, in his seventh essay:

> Some of the European nations, it's true, have provinces bordering upon us. But from these, unsupported by their European forces, we have nothing to apprehend. If any of them should attack us, they will have to transport their armies across the Atlantic, at immense expense, while we should defend ourselves in our own country, which abounds with every necessary of life.

In the second place, the Anti-Federalists argue that when defensive warfare is required, healthy republics can and should put their trust in the fighting spirit of the civilian population —organized in local, volunteer and state militias. They stress the intimidating proof that America has given to Europe—through the defeat of Great Britain in the Revolutionary War—of the defensive powers of such citizen militias. They argue, look, we have just defeated the largest empire in history in a great war through our citizen militias. There's your empirical proof that we can rely on.

Thus, Patrick Henry expostulates in one of his great orations in the Virginia Ratifying Convention, "Happily for us, there's no real danger from Europe. You may sleep in safety forever for them. Where's the danger? If there was any, I would recur to the American spirit to defend us. That spirit which has enabled us to surmount the greatest difficulties. We have the animating fortitude and persevering alacrity of republican men, to carry us through misfortunes and calamities. It's the fortune of a free people, not to be intimidated by imaginary dangers. Fear is the passion of slaves."

And here we see struck a classical keynote of the Anti-Federalist outlook. What a sound republic ought to be relying on militarily is what the great old classical republics relied on, the superior martial spirit of a virtuous republican citizenry organized and trained in local citizen militias. George Mason best articulated the argument in a speech he gave in the Constitutional Convention on June 4:

> The pervading principle in republican government is to be found in the love, the affection, the attachment of the citizens to their laws, to their freedom, and to their country. Every husbandman will be quickly converted into a soldier when he knows and feels that he is to fight not in defense of the rights of a particular family, or a prince, but his own. It was this which in ancient times enabled that little cluster of Grecian republics to resist and almost constantly to defeat, the Persian monarch. It was this which supported the states of Holland against a body of veteran troops through a thirty years war with Spain, then the greatest monarchy in Europe, and finally rendered them victorious. It is this which preserves the freedom and independence of the Swiss Cantons in the midst of the most powerful nations. And who that reflects seriously upon the situation of America, in the beginning of the late war, without soldiers, without trade, money or credit, in a manner destitute of all resources, but must ascribe our success to this pervading, all-powerful principle?

The militias, the Anti-Federalists argue, should in peacetime remain, as "The Federal Farmer" puts it in his 18th letter:

> ... solely managed [by the states,] except when called into the service of the Union ... when called into that service, they may be commanded and governed by the Union. This arrangement, [he argues,] combines energy and safety in it. It places the sword in the hands of the solid interest of the community and not in the hands of men who form the select corps. By it, the militia are the people and render regular troops in a great measure unnecessary.

"The Federal Farmer" does not and cannot deny the need for some regular or professional troops on guard duties in the border fortresses. But, like other Anti-Federalists, he warns, repeatedly and passionately, of the dangerous power, given to the federal government under this proposed constitution's Article 1, Section 8, Clause 12, of establishing a full scale standing army in peacetime—a permanent, professional, peacetime army—which the Anti-Federalists decry as the basis for a separate military establishment opposed to the interest of the civilian population.

Thus the writer who signs himself "John DeWitt," evoking the great Dutch hero of the Dutch Resistance to the Spanish, writes:

> What historians have asserted, all the Grecian republics have verified. [Professional armies] are brought up to obedience and unconditional submission ... They are excluded from the enjoyments which liberty gives to its votaries; they, in consequence, hate and envy the rest of the community ...

The most thoughtful among the Anti-Federalists cannot deny that, in the words of "The Federal Farmer," in his second letter:

> Powers nearly, if not altogether, complete and unlimited, over the purse and the sword must be lodged somewhere in every society. But, then they should be lodged where the strength and guardians of the people are collected.

That is not in the central government, but rather in state and local government. It's just too dangerous, he argues, and it isn't necessary, he insists, to bestow permanent unlimited military and taxation powers on the central government. Instead, what is prudent, he argues, is to grant the central government only limited powers in this regard, keeping the unlimited powers closer to the people in their state militias and local governments, which can, in the event of emergencies or the emergence of grave international threats, temporarily grant to the central government emergency or time-limited greater taxation or military powers.

Patrick Henry, for example, speaking in the Virginia Convention evoked the example of the Roman dictators and argued that George Washington during the Revolution was in effect a dictator. Why not adopt that model and put that into a better constitution? Keep the power of the military in the states but give a provision that in times of national emergency a dictator can be created for a temporary time period, for a certain number of months, on the model of George Washington, who will have personal power to requisition any and all troops and monies that he might need for that time period. That way you're not giving enormous powers to the government except in real emergencies and only in emergencies that the states and people all agree are real emergencies. More generally, the Anti-Federalists argue it's just too dangerous to design the powers of the central government with a view to and for the sake of possible emergencies and extreme contingencies in the distant futures, as Hamilton argues.

The Anti-Federalists stress that it's a universal experience that governments always tend to maximize whatever taxation and spending powers are given to them. Therefore it's safest to give to government at the start the least power possible. As Melancton Smith puts it, "It is a general maxim that all governments find a use for as much money as they can raise." Alexander Hamilton himself, in *Federalist* Paper 30, dares to write the following and he even puts it in italics, "I believe it may be regarded as a position, warranted by the history of mankind, that *in the usual progress of things, the necessities of a nation, in every stage of its existence, will be found at least equal to its resources.*"

Notice here that Hamilton is not saying what you might expect him to say, that a nation's resources will be enough to meet its necessities. No, he says the necessities will grow to meet the resources. In other words, he's saying whatever power a government has it will use and find a good reason for using, and then that's what's imbedded in this constitution and that's what we mean to go with. Something that seems ominous to the Anti-Federalists, that whatever a nation regards as necessary will expand with its resources and power to do what it can do. The more power a government has the more need it will find for its power.

This kind of language and thinking spurs the suspicion—which is repeatedly voiced by the Anti-Federalists, that the Federalists—in their stress on the extraordinary demands of national security, of foreign and defense policy—are not merely thinking of defense of American liberty, but are in some measure falling prey to the enchantment of visions of national glory, power, and even imperial greatness, which is a temptation, the Anti-Federalist warn, that, as Roman history proves, will sound the death-knell of small-scale republican freedom and virtue. "If we admit this Consolidated Government," Patrick Henry warns:

> ... it will be because we like a great splendid one. Some way or other we must be a great and mighty empire. We must have an army, and a navy, and a number of things. When the American spirit was in its youth, the language of America was different. Liberty, sir, was then the primary object.

Now, it's undeniably true that *The Federalist Papers* do speak of the need for a certain degree of national greatness in the international arena including—they make no bones about it—a hegemony over the entire Western hemisphere, in order, Hamilton argues, to end the European hegemony there and to keep European intervention minimal. In *Federalist* Paper 11 a paper devoted to arguing for a strong American navy, Hamilton closes with a remarkable passage, in which he pregnantly hints that he has in mind things that he is not expressing fully, things that will become clear only in the future, after the new constitutional system is underway and he practically anticipates what would later become the famous Monroe Doctrine. "I shall briefly observe," he writes,

> ... that our situation invites and our interests prompt us, to aim at an ascendant in the system of American affairs. Europe, by her arms and by her negotiations, by force and by fraud, has in different degrees, extended her dominion over Africa, Asia and America. Facts have too long supported these arrogant pretensions of the European. It belongs to us to vindicate the honor of the human race, and to teach that assuming brother moderation. Union will enable us to do it. Let Americans disdain to be the instruments of European greatness. Let the 13 states, bound together in a strict and indissoluble union, concur in erecting one great American system, superior to the control of all transatlantic force or influence and able to dictate the terms of the connection between the old and the new world!

More generally, "Publius" insists that security, both physical and financial, depends on gaining the respect of other nations, especially the European great powers. What those European powers respect above all, Hamilton says, is military and economic power, prudently managed.

In the next lecture, we will step back and evaluate this part of the Great Debate, the argument over what is required for national security and we'll see how there comes to sight here a deep dilemma that haunts the Anti-Federalists position.

# Lecture Five
# The Deep Difficulties in Each Position

**Scope:** The Federalists reply by charging the Anti-Federalists with failing to face up to what national security truly requires. Attacking as naive the exclusive reliance on state militias, "Publius" defends the need for, and the republican safety of, a professional army. The Federalists go on to raise the troubling question of whether their opponents believe wholeheartedly in a union—whether they are not really at bottom in favor of disunion. The Anti-Federalists indignantly reject this accusation and charge that the Federalist stress on defense shows a deeply mistaken ordering of priorities whereby national security takes preeminence over republican freedom in domestic life; the correct reordering of priorities requires stronger state and local governments. These levels of government have the most important tasks: citizen participation in self government, administering justice through juries, education of the young, and moral and religious regulation. In addition, in a true confederacy it is powerful state governments that can provide the balance necessary to prevent the central government from becoming a threat to liberty.

# Outline

I. To the Anti-Federalist arguments in the previous lecture, the Federalists reply by questioning forcefully whether the Anti-Federalists ever face up to what national security truly requires.

   A. The Federalists argue that the Anti-Federalists are unwilling to explain how future emergencies can be constitutionally provided or prepared for.

   B. Hamilton and Madison contend that the impracticality of the Anti-Federalist position is seen most clearly in their exclusive reliance on the militia, combined with their rejection of a small, professional peacetime army.

      1. Hamilton rejects the Anti-Federalist appeal to the model provided by the Greco-Roman citizen armies as inapplicable to the spirit and way of life of a modern, commercial society like America.

     **2.** In Papers 22 and 25, speaking from his own military experience as Washington's chief aide-de-camp, Hamilton challenges as myth the claim that the Revolution was won by relying mainly on state militia forces.

  **C.** "Publius" gives three arguments answering the fear that a professional, standing army must necessarily threaten to subvert the republic.

     **1.** The American standing army can remain quite small during peacetime, unless a grave threat looms.

     **2.** The state militias are not meant to be disbanded but are endorsed in the new constitution.

     **3.** Control over the military establishment is lodged ultimately in the hands of the legislature because it is only the legislature that is empowered to raise armies and appropriate money for them.

     **4.** The same clause forbids any money being appropriated for this purpose for a period longer than two years, thus insuring that at least every other year there will be debate in the legislature over the military budget.

**II.** This argument over the defense establishment is a powerful wedge by which "Publius" presses a deeper and broader challenge.

  **A.** Jay and Hamilton pointedly ask whether the opponents of the proposed constitution really believe in a union or whether they are not really in favor of splitting the Union into smaller, independent republics.

     **1.** Hamilton and Jay start by lodging the polemical accusation that at least some of the opponents are secretly agitating in a conspiracy to split up the United States.

     **2.** This accusation is rejected by leading Anti-Federalists, who insist that they love the Union as much as the Federalists.

  **B.** Hamilton, at the end of Paper 23, suggests that the dismemberment of the Union is not the wished for, but the necessary, implication of the Anti-Federalist argument against a consolidated Union.

     **1.** Hamilton argues that we will have to break up at least most of the existing American states because they are already too large.

     **2.** Some of the more thoughtful Anti-Federalists openly express a doubt as to whether it is possible to devise a government that is strong and unified enough to defend so vast a territory as

America without becoming a threat to republican individual freedom.

C. There is evidence showing that Anti-Federalists are vulnerable to the suggestion that their position calls into question the possibility of republican union or of the United States as a large, free republic. This is a fundamental difficulty in the Anti-Federalist position.

III. Implicit in this uncomfortable difficulty is a powerful challenge that the Anti-Federalists put to the whole Federalist position.

A. The Anti-Federalists ask if there is not something fundamentally wrong with the Federalist outlook, inasmuch as it makes national security more of a priority than the shared way of life of its citizenry.

1. The Anti-Federalists insist that one should not choose a constitutional system if the price is a serious threat of losing and endangering internal republican liberty.

2. They warn that such is exactly the trap into which the proposed constitutional system falls, on account of its deeply mistaken ordering of priorities.

B. The Federalists passionately deny that their proposed constitution and its underlying vision prioritize national security over domestic freedom; they insist that they agree with the Anti-Federalists on the fundamental ranking of priorities.

C. The Anti-Federalists argue that the Federalists should be willing to run greater risks with national security in order to leave more power in the hands of state and local governments than is allowed under the proposed constitution, both for the sake of keeping republican freedom vigorous in local self-government and for the sake of protecting that republican freedom from despotic domination by the central government.

D. State and local governments ought to have independent resources and their own taxing and military powers to carry out the more important tasks the state government has in contrast to the national government.

1. Citizen participation in self-government.

2. The administration of justice through the rule of civil and criminal law, with popular juries in charge of the courts.

3. Education of the young—especially moral and civic education.

**4.** Protecting, fostering, and regulating religious life.

**E.** The Anti-Federalists wonder how the states could check and balance so strong a central government and carry out their even greater state responsibilities if they are weakened as they are under the proposed constitution, in which the central government has unlimited military and taxation power and there is nothing approaching an equilibrium between the power of national and state governments.

**Essential Reading:**

"Agrippa" [James Winthrop], 10$^{th}$ Letter; in Storing, *The Complete Anti-Federalist*, Vol. 4, pp. 87–91.

"Brutus," Seventh Essay; in Storing, *The Complete Anti-Federalist*, Vol. 2, pp. 400–5.

"Candidus" [Samuel Adams or his follower Benjamin Austin], Second Essay; in Storing, *The Complete Anti-Federalist*, Vol. 4, pp. 130–36.

*The Federalist*, Papers 6–8, 13, and 41 (review Papers 1, 2, 11, and 23–29).

Henry, excerpts from speeches at the Virginia Ratifying Convention (June 5, 1788); in Storing, *The Complete Anti-Federalist*, Vol. 5, pp. 211–21.

"A Plebian" [Melancton Smith], opening paragraphs; in Storing, *The Complete Anti-Federalist*, Vol. 6, pp. 129–35.

**Supplementary Reading:**

Tarcov, "The Federalists and Anti-Federalists on Foreign Affairs."

————, "War and Peace in *The Federalist*."

**Questions to Consider:**

**1.** The Anti-Federalists make republican liberty and virtue in the internal life of the nation the chief priority; the Federalists make national security against foreign threats the chief priority. Which group do you think makes the more convincing argument about priorities and why?

**2.** What do you find to be the strengths and the weaknesses of the Anti-Federalist view of the needs of national security? Consider in this regard the sketches for an alternative constitution made by the Anti-Federalists "Candidus" and "Agrippa."

## Lecture Five—Transcript
## The Deep Difficulties in Each Position

At the end of the last lecture, we saw the Anti-Federalist reply to the powerful Federalist argument that asserts the need for unlimited military and hence taxation powers being vested in the central government, for the sake of national security.

The Anti-Federalists retort that the Federalists overstate the foreign dangers, at least for the foreseeable future. In the second place, the Anti-Federalists charge that the proposed constitution underestimates the efficacy and importance of military power being kept firmly rooted in local citizen militias; with a view to defense against both foreign threats and with a view to the internal threat from military despotism that would be imposed by a professional, standing national army. The proof that a state-controlled citizen militia can do the job, if local civic virtue is animated, is the fact, they say, that it was this militia that carried us through the Revolution to victory. So here again we see, as regards national security, the Anti-Federalists invoking the key role of popular virtue.

The Anti-Federalists are willing to concede that, yes, in the distant and unforeseeable future, dangerous circumstances may well arise that will require—for a time at least—a more engaged foreign policy and a more active and powerful military. But they insist it's safer to leave this to be handled in the future through emergency grants of power to the central government for temporary time periods to face dangers that are recognized by the whole people through their state governments.

To this the Federalists reply by questioning forcefully whether the Anti-Federalists then are really facing up to what national security truly requires. In effect, the Federalists say, look, you Anti-Federalists have to admit that in the future, national emergencies caused by foreign threats are almost sure to occur, but you're unwilling or unable to explain how they can be constitutionally provided or prepared for. You ask us to wait for emergencies and then concoct emergency powers. We need a constitution that gives the legal powers to government to meet any and all emergencies. Indeed, if one looks back, turning to the Anti-Federalist writings to see what exactly they sketch or propose when one looks at their alternative sketches of constitutional plans that some, among the Anti-Federalists, do indicate or layout, those for instance in the *Letters of Agrippa*, written by James Winthrop or a sketch that is developed in the essays of "Candidus," probably written by Samuel Adams or his follower Benjamin Austin. What one finds is that it's indeed striking how flimsy the provision these plans make for defense and foreign policy.

Especially revealing, Hamilton and Madison contend, of their impracticality, as well as a touch of paranoia, Hamilton says, in the whole Anti-Federalist position, is this reliance on militias that they keep harping on, combined with their rejection and from Hamilton and Madison's point of view, excessive fear, of a standing professional peacetime army, which Hamilton and Madison insist can be pretty small most of the time.

The Federalists don't deny that there is some danger to a professional peacetime army. Madison, in Paper 41, admits, in his words that, "A standing force is dangerous. But he immediately adds, "at the same time it may be a necessary provision."

Hamilton is even stronger in his attack on the attempt to rely exclusively on a citizen militia for America. Hamilton rejects this whole Anti-Federalist appeal to the model provided by the Greco-Roman citizen-armies of the great classical republics. He argues that this is really inapplicable to the spirit and way of life that is going to characterize Americans. He insists we are planning for a modern, commercial society. We are not planning for a society such as characterized early Republican Rome or Sparta or Athens or Carthage. We're thinking of a society, as he puts it in Paper 8 in which, in his words, "The industrious habits of the people of the present day, absorbed in the pursuits of gain, and devoted to the improvements of agriculture and commerce, are incompatible with the condition of a nation of soldiers, which was the true condition," he says, "of the people of those republics," meaning the Greco Roman republics.

In the second place, Hamilton challenges, as somewhat mythic, the claim made by the Anti-Federalists that the revolution was won by relying mainly on state militia forces. He admits that the militia forces fought well and made a substantial contribution, but in Papers 22 and 25, speaking from his own military experience as Washington's chief aid-de-camp for a long time, in which he served in effect as the chief of staff of the revolutionary forces, Hamilton speaks authoritatively to the effect that there was, indeed, an attempt at the beginning of the Revolution to rely exclusively on state militias, and he reminds his readers, the results proved disastrous. What resulted, he recounts, were, in his words:

> … slow and scanty levies of men, in the most critical emergencies of our affairs, short enlistments, at an unparalleled expense, continual fluctuations in the troops, ruinous to their discipline, and

subjecting the public safety frequently to the perilous crisis of a disbanded army.

In other words, Hamilton points out, these state militiamen, for all their enthusiasm, came for relatively short periods of time, had to go back home to their farms and did go back home, and on their way home, often were rather riotous. In effect, summing up, Hamilton says, "This doctrine," that is the doctrine that would rely on state militias, "had like," he says, "to have lost us our independence. It cost millions that might have been saved." In other words, it was very expensive, he says, to continually be rehiring, retraining these state militiamen.

What we really learned in the Revolution, Hamilton insists, is that, as he puts it:

> The steady operations of war against a regular and disciplined army, can only be successfully conducted by a force of the same kind … [He goes on to say] The American militia, in the course of the late war, have by their valor on numerous occasions, erected eternal monuments to their fame; but the bravest of them feel and know, that the liberty of their country could not have been established by their efforts alone, however great and valuable they were.

In other words, Hamilton points out, it was only because Washington, with the help of people like Vernon von Steuben from Europe, was finally able to create a regular national army with long enlistment periods, disciplined and kept together and organized in the way that the professional armies of Europe were organized, that he was finally able to begin to meet the British in the field and defeat them in pitch battles. Let us not forget, Hamilton said, that even all that would never have been enough to win the revolution without the very great help from the French professional navy and professional army.

In the last place, "Publius" gives three arguments answering this fear of the Anti-Federalists that a professional, standing army must necessarily threaten to subvert the republic. In the first place, Hamilton and Madison insist, especially at the end of Paper 8 and then in Paper 41, that the American standing army can remain quite small during peacetime, unless a grave threat looms. So long, that is, as the central government remains strong and energetic, because that very strength and energy will deter foreign powers. They will see that this is a government that can, whenever it wishes, enlarge its professional army through calling on the state militias.

Then, in the second place, Hamilton and Madison both stress, especially in Papers 29 and 46, that the state militias are not at all meant to be disbanded, but are emphatically and explicitly endorsed in the new constitution, in Article 1, Section 8, Clauses 15 and 16, the militia is specifically maintained and it is explicitly said that the officers of the militia are to be selected by the state governments. If these state militias, they say, are well trained and organized, they will remain there as armed citizen bodies standing as a check to the small professional army in peace time, even though they are, indeed, under the command of the central government when needed.

For, as Hamilton puts it in Paper 26, the state legislatures, in his words, "will always be not only vigilant, but suspicious and jealous guardians who can mobilize and lead popular resistance to any despotic projects based on the professional army." In this regard, "Publius" evokes, in Paper 25, what he speaks of as the healthy "jealousy," as he puts it, and "suspicion" that the populace will and ought to have toward any military establishment of the central government. Now, of course, this means that "Publius" and the Federalists claim that the Anti-Federalists' prediction that some day the militias will all be turned into some national guard that will be a centralized wing of the army are completely false. They claim that that is unconstitutional and would never happen. Here again we see, of course, a very strong place where the Anti-Federalist prediction was absolutely correct, although it took a long time to happen.

In the third place, still arguing against the danger of a professional army, "Publius" highlights the institutional mechanisms that the constitution provides within the central government to insure civilian control over the military. Control over the military, they point out, is lodged ultimately not in the hands of the President or the executive, even though he is Commander in Chief, but in the hands of the legislature, which outweighs the executive in military affairs because the constitution explicitly says that it is only the legislature that is empowered to raise armies and it is only the legislature which can appropriate money from the taxes to pay for the armies by Article 1, Section 8, Clause 12. That same clause, they point out, forbids any such money being appropriated for any military purpose for a period longer than two years. That insures, Hamilton argues, that at least every other year there will be a debate in the legislature over the military budget.

This whole argument that we have been considering, over the defense establishment, which the union requires, is one powerful wedge, by which

"Publius," *The Federalist Papers,* press a deeper and broader challenge, that they lay down to the Anti-Federalists from the very first *Federalist* paper. At this point we're in a position to understand better this challenge.

In effect, "Publius" asks his opponents the following, do you Anti-Federalists really have, can you really articulate any realistic alternative to one of two possibilities. Either we have to have this proposed constitution, with its more consolidated union, or something like it, or isn't the only other alternative splitting up the union?

"Dismemberment," as Hamilton calls it in the close of the first paper. In other words, Jay and Hamilton at the start pointedly ask whether the opponents of the proposed constitution really believe, whole-heartedly, in a union, or in a United States or whether they are not really, at heart, at bottom, in favor of disunion, splitting up the union of 13 states into some smaller independent republics.

From the outset, *The Federalist Papers* push this challenge in a manner that must strike us as being unfair and even as involving stooping to some rather low rhetorical tactics. Because from the very start, Hamilton and Jay lodge the polemical accusation, that at least some of the opponents of this proposed constitution are secretly agitating in a conspiracy to split the United States up into several smaller confederations or even into 13 independent states. Which, Hamilton then goes on in Papers 6 through 8, will likely lead to eventual war among the states or these new separate confederacies. In the long run, *that* he argues, that will lead them all to become the weak victims of European imperial interference and domination.

As one might expect, this accusation, with which *The Federalist Papers* starts, that there is a conspiracy afoot to split up the union, is indignantly rejected by the Anti-Federalists, who insist over and over again that they love the union, that they love the United States, just as much as do the Federalists. Some of the Anti-Federalists angrily retort that this whole problem, of the threat of disunion, or dismemberment, is a non-problem, a trumped up red herring. Thus "Centinel" in his eleventh letter writes, as following, "This dread of our splitting into separate confederacies or republics, that might become rival powers, is a specter that has been raised to terrify and alarm the people out of the exercise of their judgment on this great occasion. This hobgoblin," he says, "appears to have sprung from the deranged brain of "Publius" and is totally inapplicable to the subject he was professedly treating. He has wasted more paper in combating chimeras of his own creation."

Despite such justifiably angry protestations on the part of the Anti-Federalists, one can nevertheless discern an important kernel of truth underlying this unfair conspiracy charge put forth by Jay and Hamilton. Because their warnings ring a somewhat fairer and more plausible sound insofar as they express them in the more moderate way that Hamilton does at the end of Paper 23, where he suggests that the dismemberment of the union, into smaller confederacies is not the wished for, but rather the necessary, even if undesired, implication, of the Anti-Federalist argument and position against a strong, consolidated union.

Hamilton points out in the ninth Federalist paper the dilemma Americans would be put into if they followed the Anti-Federalists' appeal to Montesquieu and his vision of republics that insistence that republics must be small and participatory. If we really take that seriously, Hamilton says in the *Federalist* Paper 9, if we stick to this Montesquieuan framework, we will have to break up most of the existing states, including New York, because they're already too large. In other words, Hamilton points out, that Montesquieu is thinking of small, polis, city state like societies as one found in Greece or Rome or in the Italian states of the Middle Ages or in the Swiss Cantons. That whole model is much smaller than most of the United States except maybe Rhode Island. So if you're going to go in that direction, Hamilton says in the ninth Paper, you better plan to start splitting up states like Virginia and New York and that will be a nightmare. As Hamilton puts it:

> When Montesquieu recommends a small extent for republics, the standards he had in view were of dimensions far short of the limits of almost every one of these states. If we, therefore, receive his ideas on this point, as the criterion of truth, we shall be driven to the alternative, either of taking refuge at once in the arms of monarchy or of splitting ourselves into an infinity of little, jealous, clashing, tumultuous commonwealths, the wretched nurseries of unceasing discord, and the miserable objects of universal pity or contempt.

As a matter of fact, we do find that some of the more thoughtful of the Anti-Federalists openly express a doubt as to whether it is really possible to devise a government that is strong and unified enough, to administer so vast a territory as America without becoming, by its strength, a threat to republican and individual freedom.

Some of these Anti-Federalists are led to express reluctantly and with a kind of melancholy wonder, the question whether the insolubility of the problem might not make it necessary to break up the union into several smaller confederacies. Thus at the end of the ninth letter of "The Federal Farmer," we read,

> But if it be asked how shall we remedy the evil, so as to complete and perpetuate the temple of equal laws and equal liberty? Perhaps we can never do it. Possibly we never may be able to do it in this immense country, under any one system of laws however modified. Nevertheless, at present, I think the experiment worth a-making. I feel an aversion to the disunion of the states and to separate confederacies. Great dangers too may attend these confederacies.

One sees here in Richard Henry Lee, of course, a deep aversion to splitting up the union, yes, but a melancholy sense that that may be eventually what we have to do. But for now, no, let's try the experiment, but it's an experiment.

Similarly Patrick Henry voices the following remarkably wavering utterance. He says, "I am persuaded that separate confederacies will ruin us. In my judgment, they are evils never to be thought of till a people are driven by necessity." But then a few lines later, he says, "I am persuaded that one Government cannot reign over so extensive a country as this, without absolute despotism. Compared to such a consolidation, small Confederacies are little evils."

There is evidence showing that Anti-Federalists are vulnerable to the suggestion that their position calls into question the very possibility of republican union or of the United States as a large, free republic. This is a grave, fundamental difficulty in the whole Anti-Federalist position.

On the other hand, implicit in this deep and uncomfortable Anti-Federalist difficulty, is a powerful challenge that the Anti-Federalists, in their turn, put to the whole Federalist position. The Anti-Federalists ask, in effect, is there not something fundamentally wrong with the Federalist outlook, inasmuch as it makes national security such an overwhelming priority rather than what ought to be the preeminent priority, namely not defense, against outside forces, but the shared way of life of the citizenry inside, the way of life of freedom that makes the country worth defending. Thus "Brutus" writes, in his seventh essay:

> The preservation of internal peace and good order, and the due administration of law and justice, ought to be the first care of every government. The happiness of a people depends infinitely more on this than it does upon all that glory and respect which nations aquire by the most brilliant martial achievements and I believe history will furnish but few examples of nations who have duly attended to these, [that is the internal affairs,] who have been subdued by foreign invaders. If a proper respect and submission to the laws prevailed over all orders of men in our country and if a spirit of public and private justice, economy and industry influenced the people, we need not be under any apprehensions that they would be ready to repel any invasion that might be made on this country. And more than this, I would not wish from them a defensive war is the only one I think justifiable. The European governments are almost all of them framed and administered with a view to arms and war, as that in which their chief glory consists. They mistake the end of government. We ought to furnish the world with an example of a great people, who in their civil institutions hold chiefly in view, the attainment of virtue and happiness among ourselves.

The Anti-Federalists insist that one should not choose a constitutional system, even if it does best guarantee national security, if the price is a serious threat of losing and endangering internal republican liberty. They warn that such is exactly the trap into which this proposed constitutional system falls on account of its deeply mistaken ordering or misordering of priorities.

To this very serious charge, the Federalists reply by passionately denying that their proposed constitution and its underlying vision prioritizes national security over domestic freedom. On the contrary, they insist, they agree with the Anti-Federalists on the fundamental ranking of priorities. Hamilton states this emphatically in Paper 23, "It will indeed," he says,

> ... deserve the most vigilant and careful attention of the people, to see that our constitution be modeled in such a manner as to admit of its being safely vested with the requisite powers for national security. If any plan which has been, or may be, offered to our consideration, should not, upon a dispassionate inspection, be found to answer this description, it ought to be rejected. A

government, the constitution of which renders it unfit to be entrusted with all the powers which a free people ought to delegate to any government, would be an unsafe and improper depository of the national interests.

Madison later makes the point still more emphatically and eloquently, in both Paper 37 and then again in Paper 39. In Paper 37 Madison writes, "Among the difficulties encountered by the convention," and thus Madison sort of takes us for a moment into the convention and in effect says:

This was, let me tell you the difficulties. ... Among the difficulties encountered by the convention a very important one must have lain, in combining the requisite stability and energy in the government, with the inviolable attention due to liberty and to the republican form. Without substantially accomplishing this part of their undertaking, they would have very imperfectly fulfilled the object of their appointment or the expectation of the public.

In Paper 39, going even farther, Madison writes:

The first question that offers itself is whether the general form and aspect of the government be strictly republican? It is evident that no other form would be reconcilable with the genius of the people of America, with the fundamental principles of the Revolution or with that honorable determination which animates every votary of freedom, to rest all our political experiments on the capacity of mankind for self-government. If the plan of the convention ... therefore, be found to depart from the republican character, its advocates must abandon it, as no longer defensible.

But then, the Anti-Federalists retort, in effect:

All right, on the basis of this ranking of priorities, that you say we both agree on, shouldn't you be willing to run greater risks with national security, in foreign affairs, in order to leave much more power in the hands of state and local governments than is allowed under this proposed constitution, both for the sake of keeping republican freedom vigorous, in local self-government, administering the domestic concerns, which are the most important concerns and for the sake of protecting that republican freedom, from despotic domination by the central government, by giving state governments enough power to check and balance the central government?

As "Brutus" eloquently insists in his sixth and seventh essays directly quoting and rebutting, *Federalist* Paper 23, which I just recently mentioned, he speaks as follows, "It is as necessary, that the state governments should possess the means to attain the ends expected from them, as for the general government. Neither the general government, nor the state governments ought to be vested with all the powers proper to be exercised for promoting the ends of government. The powers are divided between them. Certain ends are to be attained by the one and other certain ends by the other, and these, taken together, include all the ends of good government. This being the case, the conclusion follows, that each should be furnished with the means, to attain the ends, to which they are designed."

Because, "Brutus" goes on to insist in the seventh essay, "... the most important end of government" as he puts it, is "the province of the state governments." He says, "that state and local governments ought to have independent resources, their own taxing and military powers, under their own control, to enable them to carry out their more important tasks." What are those more important tasks that state government has in contrast to the national government? Well, first and foremost, "Brutus says," citizen participation in self-government, especially in the militia, in the juries. Secondly, what "Brutus" calls the "Administration of justice among individuals," the rule of civil and criminal law in your local courts, with popular juries in charge. Thirdly, education of the young, especially moral and civic education of future citizens. In the fourth place, perhaps most important of all: protecting and fostering and regulating religious life which is closely linked to the protection and regulation and fostering of family life and morals. Those are the really important concerns of human life; those are the concerns that state and local government is responsible for.

Especially assuming, "Brutus" argues, that you, Federalists are right in your argument, that the central government must have these very strong powers to carry out its unique responsibilities in foreign affairs and defense and regulation of interstate commerce, how, the Anti-Federalists ask, if we're going to give those great powers to the central government, can the states check and balance them, balance such strong powers in the central government and then also carry out their own even greater state responsibilities, if they are as weakened as they are under this proposed constitution where the central government has, as you said, "unlimited" and thus, when push comes to shove, total military and taxation power, when there is nothing approaching an equilibrium or balance of power between national and state governments.

As "Brutus" protests, in his eighth essay, under this proposed constitution, he says:

> The general government have unlimited authority and control over all the wealth and all the force of the union. The advocates for this scheme would favor the world with a new discovery, if they could show what kind of freedom or independency is left to the state governments, when they cannot command any part of the property or of the force of the country, but at the will of the Congress. It seems to me as absurd, he says, as it would be to say, that I was free and independent, when I had conveyed all my property to another and was tenant to will of him, and had beside, given an indenture of myself to serve him during life.

In other words, the Anti-Federalists are asking, doesn't the proposed constitution really reduce the states to mere administrative subdivisions, under the control of this federal national government which may well allow the states considerable autonomy but which leaves all the final lawful and constitutional say to the central government, which is likely to use its constitutional powers steadily to erode and take over state power as the years go by.

In the words of a writer who signs himself "A [Pennsylvania] Farmer," "That the state governments have certain ministerial and convenient powers continued to them is not denied and in the exercise of which they may support, but cannot control the central government."

In the next lecture, we will see how this protest compels the Federalists to make clearer their conception of the federal character of their proposed constitutional order and we will see laid bare a very deep problem in that vision of federalism.

# Lecture Six
# Debating the Meaning of "Federalism"

**Scope:** The Federalists retort by insisting that they share the priority of liberty over security. We follow the elaboration of their conception of federalism (the relation between the national and state governments) in response to the Anti-Federalist critique. We see more and more clearly that the Anti-Federalists are justified in their contention that under the proposed constitutional order the state governments are to be strictly subordinated to the central government.

## Outline

I. The Anti-Federalists charge that the proposed constitution sacrifices liberty for the sake of national security, while the Federalists claim that they have devised a system that is still truly federal in that it creates a genuine division and balance of power between national and state governments.

    **A.** Madison argues that "the proposed government cannot be deemed a *national* one; since its jurisdiction extends to certain enumerated objects only, and leaves to the several states a residuary and inviolable sovereignty over all other objects."

    **B.** The Anti-Federalists voice the deeper worry that the powers as enumerated are susceptible to unforeseeably expansive interpretation in the future, especially since the power to tax is included.

II. What the Anti-Federalists come back to repeatedly is their alarm over the explicitly unlimited taxation power granted to the central government.

    **A.** In reply to this alarm, Madison suggests in Paper 45 that it is "probable" that the federal government's power to impose internal taxes will not be resorted to and that "an option will be given to the states to supply their quotas by previous collections of their own."

    **B.** Hamilton, in Paper 32, insists that "with the sole exception of duties on imports and exports," the "individual states should possess an independent and uncontrollable authority to raise their own revenues for supply of their own wants."

C. Hamilton has to concede that the national and state governments have "manifestly a co-equal and concurrent authority" to tax everything other than imports and exports, and that this might "be productive of occasional interferences in the policy" that "might require mutual forbearances."

D. This opens the key question of whether there is any real balance of constitutional power between state and federal governments that will enable the states to resist and prevent steady, lawful encroachment by the national government on state taxing power. Leading Anti-Federalists suggest the following compromise:

    1. Why not make a clear division of at least the crucial taxation power, avoiding overlap and, hence, the likelihood of conflict?

    2. Why not limit the national government's power of taxation to import and export duties and leave the powers of taxing other goods to the states, with the national government instructed to requisition from the states additional funds in the case of pressing need?

    3. There was clear evidence of the popularity of this kind of fundamental revision and compromise.

    4. In response to this suggestion, Hamilton, in Paper 30, makes his strongest statements about the incalculability of future national needs for revenue and hence the imprudence of thus limiting the national government's taxing powers.

III. In what way will there remain in the state governments any legal checking and balancing constitutional power over the national government?

A. Hamilton claims that the state legislatures "will always be not only vigilant, but suspicious and jealous guardians of the rights of citizens, against encroachments from the federal government."

B. Madison repeatedly claims that "security arises to the rights of the people," from the fact that "the different governments will control each other."

C. The Anti-Federalists wonder where in this constitution such checking power is ever granted to the states.

    1. The state governments have no constitutional or legal way to exercise any check on the federal government.

      **2.** There is no mutually controlling balance of constitutional power between state and federal governments.

      **3.** There is only the extreme, extra-constitutional check of the state governments rallying popular disobedience and resistance to the national government.

      **4.** Such extreme circumstances, rather than ongoing checking and balancing, are what Hamilton has in mind when he appeals to the "original right" of self-defense.

**D.** Madison later restates his claim that the states have checking power over the national government and points out that, prior to armed resistance and in addition to protest, the state governments can "exert their local influence in effecting a change of federal representatives … by the election of more faithful representatives."

      **1.** Does this appeal to the informal influence the state governments might have over who is elected to the federal government not underline the fact that the state governments have no formal constitutional control over the federal government?

      **2.** If the state governments are to have a reserve function in emergencies, then must not the states have some truly independent military and financial powers?

      **3.** Where are these reserve powers under this constitution?

**E.** Madison tries repeatedly to reply—in Papers 39, 43, and 45—by pointing out that state governments have a crucial role in electing the President and the Senate, to which each state sends the two senators its legislature has chosen to represent the state.

**F.** Some Anti-Federalists retort that the electors and senators are far from being the delegates of the state governments.

      **1.** The senators are not under the control or direction of their state's government.

      **2.** They are not dismissible by state government, as the delegations to Congress are under the Articles of Confederation.

**IV.** If we survey the whole argument over the nature and degree of federalism in the new constitution, it is difficult to avoid the conclusion that the Anti-Federalists have the better of this part of the debate, despite the fact that their worst predictions could be dismissed as alarmist in the short run.

**A.** In the long run, the Anti-Federalists bring out in their critique the true character and long-range implications of the proposed constitution's federalism: The new constitution seems to spell the loss of any real equilibrium between state and central levels of government.

**B.** On the other hand, we find that when the Anti-Federalists spell out their alternative of true federalism, they cannot avoid slipping back toward a league of ultimately independent states that would never lose sight of the possibility of splitting up.

**C.** The upshot of this part of the Great Debate is that there is, in principle, no tenable middle ground between true federalism (in which each of the member states retains ultimate sovereignty and the Union remains fragile) and strong national unity (in which states and localities may play subordinate roles).

**D.** The Federalists are able to avoid facing the full consequences of their constitution because they see the states are likely to retain for a long time greater hold on the allegiances of their citizens.
   **1.** Madison claims the state governments will have more public offices to fill than the national government and, hence, a larger immediate body of supporters.
   **2.** It is by state governments that "all the more domestic and personal interests of the people will be regulated and provided for."
   **3.** It is with the state governments that "the people will be more familiarly and minutely conversant."
   **4.** Both Hamilton and Madison qualify these observations by adding that, if and when the people begin to see and experience that the national government is better administered than state governments, the people will "become more partial to the federal than to the state governments."

**E.** In Paper 27, Hamilton illustrates his hope that, through the national government's effective exercise of its domestic powers, the national government will intervene and be felt by the people to be actively engaged more in the daily and local life of the nation, eclipsing the state authorities.

## Essential Reading:

"Brutus," Sixth Essay (review Seventh Essay); in Storing, *The Complete Anti-Federalist*, Vol. 2, pp. 393–405.

"The Federal Farmer," 17th letter; in Storing, *The Complete Anti-Federalist*, Vol. 2, pp. 330–39.

*The Federalist*, Papers 37, 39, 43–46, 51, 52, and 55 (review Papers 23, 26–28, 30, 32, and 35).

"A [Pennsylvania] Farmer"; in Storing, *The Complete Anti-Federalist*, Vol. 3, pp. 181–93.

## Supplementary Reading:

Diamond, *As Far As Republican Principles Will Admit*, Chapters 6, 7, and 9.

————, "What the Framers Meant by Federalism," "*The Federalist's* View of Federalism," and "*The Federalist* on Federalism."

Storing, *What the Anti-Federalists Were For*, Chapter 4.

## Questions to Consider:

1. Which of the two sides of the Great Debate do you think most legitimately can claim to be advocating true federalism and why?

2. Do you think that some version of the Anti-Federalist proposal to divide the taxing power between state and national levels of government by assigning to each, exclusively, the right to certain forms of taxation, might be feasible? Why or why not?

# Lecture Six—Transcript
## Debating the Meaning of "Federalism"

At the end of the last lecture, we saw that the Anti-Federalists charge that the proposed constitution sacrifices liberty for the sake of national security, by rendering the state governments so weak and dependent on the central government, that vigorous local self-government will be swallowed up by an overwhelming and eventually oppressive national government, against which the state governments will be too feeble to pose any effective checking and balancing.

The Federalists respond by claiming that they have devised a system that is still truly federal, in that it creates a genuine division, as well as balance, of power between national and state governments. As regards the division of powers between the state and national governments, Madison repeatedly argues that, as he puts it in Paper 39, "The proposed government cannot be deemed a *national* one; since its jurisdiction," and he's referring here to Article 1 Section 8, of the constitution, "extends," he says, "to certain enumerated objects only, and leaves to the several states, a residuary and inviolable sovereignty over all other objects."

To this claim, the Anti-Federalists respond in the first place with a simple question: Why, if that's true, wasn't that as a guarantee of this state "residual" power and "sovereignty," as you say, why was that not explicitly written into the constitution? In the second place, they voice the deeper worry, that the powers even or precisely as enumerated are susceptible of unforeseeably expansive interpretation in the future, by this national government. Thus, "Centinel" says, in his eighth letter, that the clause which "… empowers the new congress to make" and here he quotes the Constitution, "'all laws that may be necessary and proper for carrying into execution any of their powers.'" That clause, he says, "is one by virtue of which every possible law will be constitutional."

Similarly, the Pennsylvania writer who signs himself "An Old Whig" asks, "Under such a clause as this, can anything be said to be reserved and kept back from the Congress? Can it be said that Congress have no power but what is expressed? 'To make all laws which shall be necessary and proper' is, in other words, to make all such laws which the Congress shall think necessary and proper. For who shall judge, for the legislature, what is necessary and proper? Who will set themselves above the sovereign? What inferior legislature shall set itself above the supreme legislature?"

As "Brutus" says, in his fifth essay, it is "evident, that the legislature under this constitution may pass any law which they think may be proper," especially since included is the power to tax in order, as the Constitution reads, "to provide for the common defense and general welfare of the United States." "Centinel" asks:

> Now what can be more comprehensive than these words ... whatever taxes ... that they may deem requisite for the general welfare may be imposed on the citizens of these states, levied by the officers of Congress, distributed through every district in America. ... The Congress may construe every purpose for which the state legislatures now lay taxes, to be for the general welfare, and thereby seize upon every object of revenue.

This, the Anti-Federalists repeatedly point out, in a system where the final judicial tribunal that would judge all interpretations would be itself national, the federal judiciary. This is a point that Madison himself has to concede. In the same passage in Paper 39 that I quoted a moment ago, he adds:

> It is true that in controversies relating to the boundary between the two jurisdictions, [state and federal] the tribunal which is ultimately to decide, is to be established under the general government. But [he adds] this does not change the principle of the case. The decision is to be impartially made, according to the rules of the constitution: and all the usual and most effectual precautions are taken to secure this impartiality. Some such tribunal is clearly essential [he says] to prevent an appeal to the sword and a dissolution of the social compact; and that it ought to be established under the general, rather than under the local governments; or, to speak more properly, that it could be safely established under the first alone, is a position not likely to be combated. [Madison says.]

But of course, it is combated, as we shall see even more vividly when we get to the fight over the judiciary. The supreme power of this federal judiciary is a key part of what the Anti-Federalists are combating.

What the Anti-Federalists come back to over and over again is their alarm over the explicitly unlimited taxation power granted to this central government. As "Brutus" writes in his seventh essay:

> Where the powers are divided between the general and the state government, it is essential to its existence, that the revenues of the country, without which no government can exist, should be divided

between them, and so apportioned to each, as far as human wisdom can effect such a division and apportionment. It has been shown, that no such allotment is made in this constitution, but that every source of revenue is under the control of the Congress; it therefore follows, that if this system is intended to be a complex and not a simple, a confederate and not an entire consolidated government, it contains in it the sure seeds of its own dissolution.

Now, in reply to this alarm, Madison suggests in Paper 45 that it is "probable," as he puts it, that the federal government's power to impose internal taxes, in addition to duties on foreign imports "will not be resorted to," Madison claims, "except for supplemental purposes," and, he promises, "an option will then be given to the States to supply their quotas by previous collections of their own." This, of course, turned out to be completely false. Madison promised that under the constitution most of the taxation would just be import and export duties at the federal level, and that if the federal government ever did get into any other taxation it would first give the states the option of paying requisitions. That, of course, never happened. Once again, the Anti-Federalists were exactly right, that the taxation power of the federal government would spread.

Similarly, Hamilton, in his discussion of the taxing power in *Paper* 32, insists that, as he puts it, "With the sole exception of duties on imports and exports, the individual States should possess an independent and uncontrolable authority to raise their own revenues for the supply of their own wants." Yet, in the same breath and in some amazing double talk, Hamilton has to concede that the national and state governments have, as he puts it, "manifestly a coequal and concurrent authority" to tax everything that's not imports and exports. He admits this "might," in his words, "be productive of occasional interferences in the policy," which as he puts it, "might require [mutual] forbearances." Now, is this not a somewhat deceptive way of referring to conflicts? Thereby opening the key question, whether there is any real balance of constitutional power between state and federal governments, such as will enable the states to resist and prevent steady lawful encroachment by the national government on the state taxing power in its reach.

As Hamilton notes in papers 30 and then 35, those he calls "the more intelligent adversaries of the new constitution" have pressed the following compromise suggestion, as the basis of a new, revised constitution. Why not, they say, convene a new convention and in a new constitution make a clear explicit division of the crucial taxation power, avoiding overlap and hence a likelihood of interference and conflict? Why not limit the national government's power of taxation to specific items—for example, all import and export duties—and leave the powers of taxing other goods to the states, with the national government instructed to requisition, from the states, additional funds in case of pressing need? Would not some such arrangement of a clear distribution of what can be taxed by each level of government express a more truly balanced, truly federal system?

This indeed was one of the amendments that the Massachusetts ratification included as recommended, and this recommendation was then followed by other states in their ratifications. In other words, it was very clear that this was a very popular compromise suggestion. It's in response to this suggestion, that Hamilton, in *Paper* 30, makes some of his strongest statements about the incalculability of future national needs for revenue and hence the imprudence of thus limiting the national government's taxing and other powers.

But then in what way will there remain in the state governments any legal checking and balancing constitutional power over this national government? Hamilton claims that, in his words in Paper 26, the state legislatures, he says, "... will always be not only vigilant, but suspicious and jealous guardians of the rights of the citizens, against encroachments from the federal government." Following Hamilton's lead, Madison repeatedly claims, in papers 51, then in 52, and then in 55, that, as he puts it, "security arises to the rights of the people" from the fact that "the different governments will control each other." As he goes on to put it, "in the compound republic of America, the power surrendered by the people is first divided between two distinct governments ... the federal legislature will not only be restrained by its dependence on the people, as other legislative bodies are, but it will be moreover watched and controlled by the several collateral [state] legislatures ... which must feel so many motives to watch, and which possess so many means of counteracting the federal legislature ..." To which the Anti-Federalists ask, what means are you talking about? Where in this constitution is such checking power ever granted to a state legislature, or to all the state legislatures?

As is pointed out by "Brutus" in his 10th essay, the state governments have no constitutional or legal way to exercise any check on the federal government. There is no mutually controlling balance of constitutional power between state and federal governments. There is no equilibrium in this document exercised in the regular course of civil and lawful government. Rather, the only thing that's left is the extreme, extra-constitutional check of the state governments rallying popular disobedience and resistance to the national government, starting civil strife, a civil war, in terrible times of emergency, when the national government has undertaken unpopular and unconstitutional usurpation of its lawful authority. That such extreme circumstances, rather than an ongoing lawful constitutional checking and balancing, is indeed what Hamilton at least has in mind, is confirmed by the way Hamilton himself subsequently speaks of this, in Paper 28, when he appeals to what he calls, in his words, "… that original right of self-defence which is paramount to all positive forms of government; and which, against the usurpation of the national rulers, may be exerted by the states." Then in Paper 60, Hamilton refers to "… an immediate revolt of the great body of the people, headed and directed by the state governments," as the means of checking the central government.

Similar revolutionary or civil war language, with a similar meaning, is found in Madison's later restatement of his claim that the states have a checking power over the national government. As Madison puts it in Paper 46:

> Ambitious encroachments of the federal government, on the authority of the State governments, would not excite the opposition of a single State, or of a few States only. They would be signals of general alarm. Every government would espouse the common cause. A correspondence would be opened. Plans of resistance would be concerted. [He says.] One spirit would animate and conduct the whole. The same combination, in short, would result from an apprehension of the federal, as was produced by the dread of a foreign yoke.

In other words, it would be just like the Revolutionary War again, but not against England, now against the federal government. He goes on, "unless the projected innovations should be voluntarily renounced," that is, by the federal government, "the same appeal to a trial of force would be made in the one case, as was made in the other."

The only thing Madison adds is that prior to this armed resistance, which would be the ultimate check the states could use, and in addition to protesting, the state governments could also, as he puts it in Paper 44, "… exert their local influence in effecting a change of federal representatives"—"by the election of more faithful representatives." But does this appeal to the informal influence of the state governments in federal elections, the influence they might have over who is being elected to the federal government, not underlying the fact that the state governments have no direct or formal constitutional control over the federal government?

If the state governments are to have even this reserve, last-ditch, extra-constitutional, revolutionary function, in emergencies, of arousing the people in civil war, well then, the Anti-Federalists ask, must not the states have some truly independent military, and therefore financial, powers in order to arm the people when they bring them out into the streets? Hamilton seems to concede this, for he goes on in Paper 28 to speak of the needs that "The people be," as he puts it, "in a situation, through the medium of their state governments, to take measures for their own defence, with all the celerity, regularity, and system, of independent nations." That last phrase is remarkable. Because does not that language suggest that the state governments must hold in reserve powers that are sufficient, to make them capable of becoming, at least in emergencies, like "independent nations," as Hamilton says, capable of fighting the central government? But, where are these reserve powers, under this constitution, ask the Anti-Federalists?

More specifically, they ask, are not the militias to be put under the authority and direction of the national government, to almost whatever degree the latter wishes? See Article 1, Section 8, Clause 16. As regards taxation and all other national powers, are not all state officials to be made subordinate and auxiliary to national authority, which can employ and command them as it wishes? Does not "Publius" himself point this out, in Paper 27, when he says, and these are his words:

> The plan reported by the convention, by extending the authority of the federal head to the individual citizens of the several States, will enable the government to employ the ordinary magistracy of each state, in the execution of its [that is, the federal] laws. [And he goes on to say:] It is easy to perceive this will tend to destroy, in the common apprehension, all distinction between the sources from which they might proceed ... Thus [he goes on to admit] the legislatures, the courts, and magistrates, of the respective members, will be incorporated into the operations of the national government as far as its just and constitutional authority extends; and will be rendered auxiliary to the enforcement of its [that is, the federal] laws.

The Anti-Federalists simply ask, doesn't this passage confirm our worst suspicions? "The Federal Farmer" puts the Anti-Federalist point incisively, at the end of his 17th letter:

> I have often heard it observed [he writes] that ... the state governments will be the people's ready advocates. ... But of what avail will these circumstances be, if the state governments, thus allowed to be the guardians of the people, possess no kind of power, by the forms of the social compact, to stop, in their passage, the laws of Congress injurious to the people?

Madison tries repeatedly to reply, in Papers 39, 43, 45, and 62. He knows that he's on the ropes on this issue, and he constantly tries to come back with arguments. The argument he makes in these four papers that I have mentioned are to say, well, the state governments have a crucial role in electing the President, through the electoral college that we've devised. Also, above all, they have great power through the Senate, because in the Senate, each state will send two senators chosen by its legislature as its representatives.

The shrewdest of the Anti-Federalists, looking at this argument, cogently retort that the electors in the electoral college and the senators are far from being delegates of the state governments. They are not under the orders of the state governments. The senators, once they are selected, are in no way under the control or direction of the state governments. The most obvious sign of that, the Anti-Federalist says, is that they can't be dismissed by the state governments—just like the electors can't be dismissed—as the delegations to the Congress under the existing Articles of Confederation can be dismissed. There, the Anti-Federalists argue, pointing to the Articles of Confederation, there you have real state control, when the people sent to Congress can be hired and fired by the state governments. That's not true of the senators. In the words of "A [Pennsylvania] Farmer":

> The exercise of sovereignty does not consist in choosing masters, such as the senators would be, who, when chosen, would be beyond control, but in the power of dismissing, impeaching, or the like, those to whom authority is delegated.

If we step back now and survey the whole argument about the nature and the degree of federalism in the new constitution, I think it's difficult to avoid the conclusion that the Anti-Federalists have the better of this part of the debate, despite the fact that their worst predictions could be dismissed as alarmist in the short run. What they warn of turned out to be mostly exaggerated in the short run or as regards the first decades, at least, of American history. But in the long run, much of what they predicted came true. The state militias have been dissolved in effect and incorporated into a national guard that is just a wing of the national military. The interstate commerce provisions of the constitution have allowed the national government to take control of and regulate commerce everywhere within the states. One of the most outrageous predictions of the Anti-Federalists, that was laughed at at the time, was that someday there might even be federal taxes on income. That of course, required a constitutional amendment, but it was an amendment that, at the time, was plausibly argued to be in the spirit of this constitution, a spirit which the Anti-Federalists pointed out.

As regards to the long run, the Anti-Federalists bring out in their critique the true character and long-range implications of this proposed constitution's federalism. The new constitution does seem to spell the loss of any real equilibrium or balance of power between the state and the central levels of government. Yet, on the other hand, we find that when the Anti-Federalists spell out their alternative of true federalism, or when they explain what sort of constitutional system would be required—when, for example, as we've seen, they propose a real division of the powers of taxation and say that the federal government should only have the power to tax exports and imports through duties; whenever they try to explain how you can have a system where the state governments genuinely counterbalance, through reserve powers in the constitution, the power of the federal government—we find that they can't avoid slipping back toward some form of a mere league, of ultimately independent states, who would never lose sight of the possibility of splitting up or going their own separate ways.

Thus, for example, the "[Pennsylvania] Farmer," who articulates one of the most theoretically sophisticated Anti-Federalist discussions of the nature of true federalism, writes:

> The perfection of a federal republic consists in drawing the proper line … reserving such a proportion of sovereignty in the state governments as would enable them to exist alone, if the general government should fail, either by violence or with the common consent of the confederates; the states should respectively have laws, courts, force, and revenues of their own, sufficient for their own security; they ought to be fit to keep house alone if necessary.

This of course means that the union would be one in which each member state would constantly have to prepare to be able to go it alone, as an independent nation. Can a unified country be built on such a basis?

The upshot of this part of the Great Debate would seem to be that there is really in principle no tenable middle ground between either true federalism, in which each of the member states retains ultimate sovereignty and union remains fragile, or national union, in which states as well as localities may play important but ultimately subordinate and ministerial roles.

The Federalists want to obscure this fundamental truth, this necessarily exclusive alternative. The Federalists fail to face this fundamental truth either because they don't wish to face the full consolidating consequences of their constitution or because they wish, as the Anti-Federalists charge, to hide this truth from the people. Or perhaps it's most likely that their true motives are a mixture of these two. It's not unlikely that, in the light of the deep split that occurred a few years later between Hamilton and Madison on precisely this issue, on the meaning of the federalism that was intended by the constitution, there may be some submerged disagreement in this respect between Hamilton and Madison. It's not implausible to suspect that Madison was less aware of the full consequences of this constitution and that Hamilton was more fully aware, more clear-sighted, and more inclined to try to hide what he saw were the consequences.

The Federalists are able to avoid facing the full consolidating consequences of their proposed constitution partly because they see and they say that the states are likely for at least a long time to retain greater hold on the affections and allegiances of their citizens. In Papers 45 and 46, Madison gives the reasons for this, enlarging on what Hamilton said back in Paper 17 and drawing on key points made by the Anti-Federalists themselves. In the first place, Madison claims, the state governments will have many more public offices to fill than will the national government, at least for a time, and hence a larger immediate body of patronage supporters. More importantly, it's by the state governments that, as he puts it "all the more domestic and personal interests of the people will be regulated and provided for," at least for a long time. Then, thirdly, it is with the state governments that, in Madison's words, "the people will be more familiarly and minutely conversant. With the members of these, will [have] a greater proportion of the people … ties of personal acquaintance and friendship, and of family and party attachments."

Yet, both Hamilton and Madison go on to qualify considerably these observations, by adding the thought that if and when the people begin to see and experience that the national government is much better administered than their state and local governments, as Hamilton and Madison expect it will be, then the people will, in Madison's words, "become more partial to the federal than to the state governments."

In Paper 27, Hamilton summarizes a number of strong reasons, that we will see laid out by Madison in the *Federalist* Paper 10, why it is, in Hamilton's words, the case that "the general government will be better administered than the particular governments." Then Hamilton proceeds to write the following very revealing passage:

> ... as the operations of the national authority are intermingled in the ordinary exercise of government; the more the citizens are accustomed to meet with it [that is, the national government] in the common occurrences of their political life; the more it is familiarized to their sight, and to their feelings; the further it enters into those objects, which touch the most sensible chords, and put in motion the most active springs of the human heart; ... the greater will be the probability, that ... the authority of the union, and the affections of the citizens towards it, will be strengthened, rather than weakened, by its extension to what are called matters of internal concern.

Here I think one can say we catch a glimpse of Hamilton's long-range hope, that through the national government's effective exercise of its domestic powers, perhaps especially over commerce and the national economy, the national government will intervene and be felt more by the people to be actively engaged in the daily and local life of the nation, eclipsing, taking over in some measure, the state authorities. A passage such as this lends some credence to the suspicion voiced most pointedly by Luther Martin, the attorney general of Maryland, who had been a delegate to the convention and who decried the proposed constitution. In these words, he says it has:

> Just so much federal in appearance as to give its advocates in some measure, an opportunity of passing it as such upon the unsuspecting multitude, before they had time and opportunity to examine it, and yet so predominantly national as to put it in the powers of its movers, whenever the machine shall be set agoing, to strike out every part that has the appearance of being federal, and to render it wholly and entirely a national government.

In the next lecture, we will see how the outcome of this argument, over the character of the proposed constitution's federalism, puts before us a fundamental question, which prepares us to appreciate fully how new and unclassical is this Federalist or Madisonian conception of internal republican liberty.

# Lecture Seven
# The Madisonian Republic

**Scope:** Since the Federalists do not propose a balancing equilibrium between state and national governments, what do they propose to substitute as a means of preventing despotic power in the central government? The cornerstone of the Madisonian answer is the argument for the rejection of the classical republican ideal in the name of a new counter-ideal: the superior liberty and security of a vast, representative republic animated by fierce competition among mutually hostile "factions" or "parties" (what we would today call "interest groups"). Madison identifies majority faction as the overriding danger in republics; all earlier democratic republics have self-destructed because the majority coalesced into a single party led by demagogues that proceeded to oppress minorities and plunge the society into class warfare. The new extended, commercial republican society, however, will be so diverse in its array of competing minority factions that the coalescence of a majority faction is rendered unlikely; what is more, this new kind of republic will be so populous that the vast majority cannot have any direct role in government, which thus becomes entirely representative, and elected representatives can be expected to possess distinguished civic virtue. The Madisonian vision thus continues, in its own way, a major moral dimension of the classical tradition in its more aristocratic, less populist, version.

# Outline

I.  The debate over the character and ultimate meaning of the proposed constitution's federalism leads to the question: If the proposed constitution does not rely mainly on the checks and balances of federalism to prevent the national government from becoming despotic, what do the Federalists and the constitution rely upon?

II. Papers 9 and 10 provide the foundation of the answer to this question, which makes clearer the radically new and unclassical character of the Federalists' republican vision.

A. Hamilton and Madison insert a short but pregnant argument for the decisive superiority of a massive national republic whose government is far removed from the direct control of the people.

B. They make this positive argument on the basis of a negative argument for the drastic inferiority of the small, homogenous, and more participatory democracy. This argument begins with a frontal attack on classical republicanism.
   1. Classical republics are famous for their unending class warfare between rich and poor.
   2. When we look at the actual history of classical republics, Hamilton points out, what we find is that popular rule and participation in self-government led to fratricidal strife rather than community.
   3. The individual virtues of Greece and Rome were not promoted but instead perverted by "the vices of government" that pervaded classical republicanism.

C. In *Federalist* 10, Madison elaborates on what is at the heart of these vices: the "violence of faction."
   1. Republics perish under this vice and this same fate threatens the 13 American states.
   2. Faction, for Madison, implies the predominance of passions and interests that move groups of citizens in ways that threaten the rights of other citizens or the good of the whole community.

D. Madison contends that the proposed constitution frames the first kind of republic in all of human history that has an effective tendency "to break and control the violence of faction."

III. The new, unclassical spirit of the proposed constitution becomes clearer when we follow Madison's argument as to exactly how this "breaking and controlling of the violence of faction" is to be accomplished.

A. Madison begins by submitting that there are two methods of "curing the mischiefs of factions": removing their causes and controlling their effects.
   1. Removing the causes means somehow preventing factions from becoming major factors in civic life, and there are only two ways of accomplishing this: despotically doing away with liberty and trying to make the populace a fraternal community.

2. The proposed constitution is based on the deep premise that any attempt to form a fraternal community is against human nature.

B. Madison spells out the reasons why factionalism is embedded in human nature.
    1. Human reason is driven mainly by what he calls "self-love."
    2. The one form of self-love he spotlights is the economic form, expressed in the love of acquiring property.
    3. When government succeeds in its prime purpose, which is to protect the acquisitive faculties of the citizens, the necessary result is the emergence of "different degrees and kinds of property" and thereby great economic diversity and inequality among the citizenry.
    4. Madison stresses a "zeal for different opinions concerning religion," including a zealotry for conflicting political opinions.
    5. Madison never adopts a biblical outlook: He never ascribes factionalism to sinfulness or human choice; rather, he says that this is the fixed and unalterable nature of humans.

C. Madison's view of humanity's social nature is not simply dark, however, but complex and subtle.
    1. Madison does not rule out some important role for "enlightened statesmen" but insists that they will "rarely prevail over the immediate interest which one party may find in disregarding the rights of another, or the good of the whole."
    2. Madison later makes it clear that in Paper 10 he has abstracted somewhat from the fraternal impulses that he is well aware manifest themselves in human nature and that have some unusual strength among Americans.
    3. While Madison does not deny the existence of deep bonds of kinship among Americans, he contends that such bonds are not strong enough to prevent the natural emergence of even stronger factional competition.

D. Madison declares that the new constitution "involves the spirit of party and faction in the necessary and ordinary operations of government." This reveals the direction that Madison and the new republic are going to take.

1. The "spirit of faction" is going to be accepted as a necessary and routine aspect of American republican government.
2. Faction itself will be the primary tool to combat and control faction.
3. The new American regime is going to be the first republic in history that is going to tolerate, foster, and depend upon mutually antagonistic competition among selfish groups seeking to exploit one another throughout society and inside the government.

E. Madison's next step is to argue that once we have admitted this basic truth, we have to realize that in a republican form of society the most serious danger is from the majority, if and when it becomes unified as a faction.
   1. Since the majority has the greatest power, it can defeat all minority factions.
   2. Who or what can check the majority if or when it becomes a unified faction?
   3. This problem is the great problem with republics that has never been solved and is why the cause of republicanism has fallen into disrepute.

IV. The solution to this problem is, according to Madison, "the great object to which our inquiries are directed." He poses the question of how one can attain this object.

A. One of two things must happen: either "the existence of the same passion of interest in a majority, at the same time, must be prevented," or "the majority, having such co-existent passion or interest, must be rendered, by their number and local situation, unable to concert and carry into effect schemes of oppression."

B. In order for these effects to happen, we must emphatically avoid setting up what Madison calls a "pure democracy": "a society consisting of a small number of citizens, who assemble and administer the government in person."
   1. In such a society, the assembled majority has direct political power and will easily coalesce into a unified faction.
   2. Madison contradicts a basic premise of the Anti-Federalist vision by denying that participatory democracies foster republican liberty.

3. Madison insists that historical evidence shows that such democracies endanger the liberty of individuals and minorities through tyranny of the majority as a faction.

C. What we must set up instead of a democracy in the classical sense is what Madison calls a republic: "a government in which the scheme of representation takes place."

V. The real heart of the new Madisonian republican vision is that the new American constitution aims not at a confederacy of small, democratic republics but instead at one large mass republic in which the people can never assemble to govern directly and in which the majority can never unite and become directly oppressive of minorities and individuals.

A. The most important consideration in this regard is the fact that the majority will be so diverse and riven by conflicting factional interests that it will rarely share the same interests.

B. Madison stands the Anti-Federalist argument on its head in two major respects.
1. Where the Anti-Federalists follow classical republican theory in seeking homogeneity of the populace, Madison sees clashing diversity as the key to maintaining liberty in a republic.
2. Where the Anti-Federalists worry about the distancing of representatives from the people and the people's control, it is this removal that Madison sees as a key to safe, effective representative government.

**Essential Reading:**

*The Federalist*, Papers 10 and 14 (review Papers 2, 9, 17, 27, 37, 39, 45, and 46).

**Supplementary Reading:**

Epstein, *The Political Theory of "The Federalist,"* Chapter 3.

Storing, *What the Anti-Federalists Were For*, Chapter 5.

**Questions to Consider:**

1. Do you find that Madison's argument decisively proves the superiority of his republican vision to the republican vision of the Anti-Federalists, or not—and why or why not?

2. Exactly what does Madison mean by "faction" and what are his arguments against the classical republican attempt to cure the "violence of faction" by preventing faction from predominating in a republican society?

# Lecture Seven—Transcript
## The Madisonian Republic

In the last lecture, we followed out the debate over the character and ultimate meaning of the proposed constitution's federalism. We saw how this part of the debate reveals the degree to which the proposed constitution, as the Anti-Federalists correctly warn, creates a system in which the national government will eventually have overwhelming power.

We're thus in a position to appreciate fully the weight of the big question, to which this leads: If or insofar as it's now become clear that the proposed constitution does not and cannot rely mainly on the checks and balances of federalism to prevent the national government, with its unlimited and overwhelming military and taxation powers, from becoming despotic, then upon what do the Federalists, and this constitution, rely? What do the Federalists propose to substitute for federalism as the source of checks and balances for the central government, and thus protection for republican liberty?

This puts us in the best position to see how *The Federalist*, Papers 9 and 10 provide the foundation of the answer to this crux question, an answer that makes still clearer the radically new and deeply unclassical character of the Federalists' republican vision. For while the bulk of the first third of *The Federalist Papers* make the case for the proposed constitution on the grounds of national security, Hamilton and Madison do insert, in Papers 9 and 10, a short but pregnant argument, on grounds of internal republican liberty, for the decisive superiority of a massive, large, national republic, whose government is far removed from the direct control of the people. They make this positive argument for their new system on the basis of a negative argument against the drastic inferiority of the small, homogeneous, and more direct or participatory democracy that is the polestar of the classical republican tradition.

This negative argument begins from that frontal attack on classical republicanism which we saw Hamilton starts off *The Federalist* Paper 9 with, and that I read in an earlier lecture. Recall Hamilton's searing words, "It is impossible to read the history of the petty republics of Greece and Italy, without feeling sensations of horror and disgust at the distractions with which they were continually agitated, and at the rapid succession of revolutions, by which they were kept perpetually vibrating between the extremes of tyranny and anarchy." Hamilton, who is then seconded by Madison in the next, or Paper 10, spotlights the fact that the classical republics, and not least the

Roman, are famous for their unending class warfare between rich and poor, or "patricians and plebeians," as Hamilton puts it later, in Paper 70.

When we look at the actual history of the classical republics, Hamilton points out, what we find is that direct, popular rule and participation in self-government lead more often than not to fratricidal strife, rather than fraternal community. Hamilton does not deny that Greece and Rome, as he puts it, "have been justly celebrated" for "producing bright talents and exalted endowments," but, he contends, these individual virtues were not promoted, but were instead "perverted," as he says, by what he calls "the vices of government" that pervaded classical republicanism.

In Paper 10, Madison elaborates on what is at the heart of these vices. That is what Madison calls, following Hamilton, the "violence of faction." It is "this dangerous vice," in Madison's words, that is to be regarded as the source of what he calls "the mortal diseases under which popular governments have everywhere perished." Hence, Madison says, in his words:

> The friend of popular governments never finds himself so much alarmed for their character and fate as when he contemplates their propensity to this dangerous vice. The violence of faction everywhere ... republics perish under this vice. There are no exceptions.

He goes on to say that this same fate threatens the 13 American states. It is, Madison writes, the "unsteadiness and injustice, with which a factious spirit has tainted our public administrations," in all thirteen states, which, he says, is the chief cause of what he calls "that prevailing and increasing distrust of public engagements, and alarm for private rights, which are echoed from one end of the continent to the other." Then, Madison defines very precisely just what he means by "faction."

> By a faction, [he writes] I understand a number of citizens, whether amounting to a majority or minority of the whole, who are united and actuated by some common impulse of passion, or of interest, adverse to the rights of other citizens, or to the permanent and aggregate interests of the community.

So "faction" for Madison implies the predominance of passions and interests that move groups of citizens in ways that threaten injury to the rights of other citizens or to the good of the whole community. It's crucial that we keep this precise and quite pejorative definition of faction firmly in mind as we follow now Madison's argument through *The Federalist* Paper 10, or otherwise we won't see how radical and even shocking his argument is.

Madison contends that this proposed new constitution frames the first kind of republic in all of human history which has an effective "tendency," as he puts it, "to break and control the violence of faction." The new, unclassical spirit of the proposed constitution becomes clearer when we follow Madison's argument as to exactly how this "breaking and controlling of the violence of faction" is to be accomplished.

Madison begins by submitting that there are, as he puts it, only "two methods of curing the mischiefs of faction. The one," he says, "by removing its causes; the other, by controlling its effects." The first method, removing the causes, means somehow preventing factions from becoming major factors in civic life, and there are only two ways of accomplishing this, Madison goes on to explain. The first is despotically doing away with liberty and thus preventing citizens from being able even to form politically effective "interest groups" which would attempt to dominate or exploit one another. This suppression of groups is of course out of the question for Americans.

The second way is to take the path of the classical republican tradition. That is, to try to make the populace homogeneous in its outlook, a fraternal community. Or, in Madison's words, by "giving to every citizen the same opinions, the same passions, and the same interests." This, Madison goes on to make eloquently clear, is what the proposed constitution rejects as "impracticable."

The proposed constitution is based on the deep premise that any attempt to build a fraternal community of public spirited citizens sharing the same outlook is simply against human nature. As Madison puts it, "The latent causes of faction are thus sown in the nature of man; and we see them every where," he says, "brought into different degrees of activity, according to the different circumstances of civil society."

Madison spells out in detail the reasons why factionalism or mutually exploitative group conflict is embedded in human nature. To begin with, and most generally, human reason is necessarily driven mainly, though not exclusively, by what Madison calls "self-love." While self-love takes many forms, there is one form that Madison spotlights above all. The economic form, expressed in the love of "acquiring," as he puts it, ever more and more property—this limitless acquisitive drive is so natural to mankind that

Madison goes so far as to declare that, in his words, "The first object of government is the protection of these faculties ... from which the rights of property originate."

Then Madison observes that when government succeeds in this prime purpose of protecting the acquisitive, selfish faculties, the necessary result is the emergence of what Madison calls "different degrees and kinds of property" and thereby great economic diversity, and great economic inequality, among the citizenry. For, Madison now adds, these faculties of acquiring property are themselves unequal or unequally distributed. This, Madison continues, necessarily divides society into mutually opposed "parties" or "factions." As Madison puts it, "From the protection of different and unequal faculties of acquiring property, the possession of different degrees and kinds of property immediately results; and from the influence of these on the sentiments and views of the respective proprietors, ensues a division of the society into different interests and parties."

It's not only the competing economic interests that necessarily split human society into warring factions. Madison stresses also what he calls "a zeal for different opinions concerning religion" as the first in a list of differences of opinion that always have this effect, of creating factions of mutually hostile groups. The list includes also zealotry for conflicting political opinions, but also zealotry for all sorts of other opinions, in theory and in practice. In addition, again in Madison's words, "attachment to different leaders, ambitiously contending for preeminence and power." All these different sorts of hostile attachments "... have, in turn," Madison writes, "divided mankind into parties, inflamed them with mutual animosity, and rendered them much more disposed to vex and oppress each other, than to co-operate for their common good."

Madison's presentation of human nature grows still darker when he adds— these are his words—"So strong is this propensity of mankind, to fall into mutual animosities, that where no substantial occasion presents itself, the most frivolous and fanciful distinctions have been sufficient to kindle their unfriendly passions, and excite their most violent conflicts." In other words, humans are by nature so eager to hurt one another and even to kill one another, that they will start doing so at almost any excuse.

Notice that Madison never says that this is a sign of human sin or sinfulness, or the fall. He does not for a moment adopt a biblical outlook. Madison says rather that this is the fixed and unalterable nature of humans, something for which humans are not responsible. He never suggests that the proper response or remedy is prayer or hope for divine redemption.

We must not leap to the conclusion that Madison's view of humanity's social nature is unrelievedly dark, a Hobbesian war of all against all. His conception is more complex and subtle. In the first place, Madison here indicates that he is not ruling out some important role for what he calls "enlightened statesmen." He insists that such statesmen will, as he puts it, "… rarely prevail over the immediate interest which one party may find in disregarding the rights of another, or the good of the whole."

Then in the second place, Madison makes it clear a few papers later in Paper 14, that he has in this Paper 10, abstracted somewhat from the communal or fraternal impulses that he is well aware do also manifest themselves in human nature; impulses which he recognizes have some unusual strength among Americans. Echoing Jay's second paper, Madison writes in Paper 14:

> Hearken not to the unnatural voice, which tells you that the people of America, knit together as they are by so many chords of affection, can no longer live together as members of the same family; can no longer continue the mutual guardians of their mutual happiness. … The kindred blood which flows in the veins of American citizens, the mingled blood which they have shed in defense of their sacred rights, consecrate their union, and excite horror at the idea of their becoming aliens, rivals, enemies.

So, while Madison thus does not deny the existence of some deep and strong bonds of kinship and affection uniting people and especially Americans, he does contend, in effect, that such natural bonds are by no means strong enough to prevent the equally or more natural emergence of even stronger fierce and mutually hurtful factional competition.

In *The Federalist* Paper 10, Madison returns to economic competition as the most powerful source of the natural mutual hatred and animosity that overwhelms kinship and public spirit. As he puts it:

> The most common and durable source of factions, has been the various and unequal distribution of property. Those who hold, and those who are without property … those who are creditors, and those who are debtors … a landed interest, a manufacturing interest, a mercantile interest, a monied interest, with many lesser interests, grow up of necessity in civilized

nations ,and divide them into different classes, actuated by different sentiments and views. ....

The regulation [he goes on to say] of these various and interfering interests forms the principal task of modern legislation, and [now listen carefully to this] involves the spirit of party and faction in the necessary and ordinary operations of Government.

This last phrase is pregnant and the most important phrase in the entire *Federalist* papers, because you see what it means and it reveals the direction that Madison and the new kind of republic are going to take. In their new solution to the problem of faction, "the spirit of faction," or what he calls "mutual animosity," is going to be accepted as a routine, intrinsic, and even necessary part of American republican government. Faction is going to be used as the primary tool to combat and control faction. The new American republic will fight fire with fire. This new system is rooted in a kind of judo-throw, if you will. Faction will itself be used to check faction; the disease will be turned back upon itself. The new American republic is to be the first republic in history that is frankly going to tolerate and even to foster and in some measure to depend upon promoting faction, mutually antagonistic competition, among selfish groups seeking to exploit one another, throughout society and inside the government itself.

What classical republicanism sought to prevent or repress, the new American republicanism is going to employ as an engine of its energetic thriving. Madison's next step is to argue that once we have admitted this basic and rather grim truth, we have to realize that in a republican form of society, where the majority has the preponderant power, where the majority is the legitimate source of authority, the most serious danger is not from any minority faction, but rather from the majority, if and when it becomes united as a faction. Since the majority has the greatest power and the greatest legitimacy, it can defeat, in the long run, and overawe or check on a regular basis, all minority factions. But who or what can check the majority, if or when it becomes a united single faction? Which, as the experience of the failure of classical republicanism shows, is most likely, and most pernicious, when the majority, who are always the poorer, unite in resentment against the wealthier, who are always the fewer, and proceed, often under the stimulus of demagogues, to place the rights of property under such threats, that either the economy is ruined or the propertied class are impelled to fight back in ruinous civil conflict.

It's this problem, of majority faction, that is the great problem with all past republics that has never before been solved. This is why the cause of republicanism has fallen into disrepute, Madison says. So it's the solution of this problem, the problem of majoritarian faction, which, in Madison's words, "is then the great object to which our inquiries are directed." Then Madison poses the $64 question: "By what means is this object attainable?"

Madison immediately proceeds to give the answer in principle. One of two things, or both at once, must be made to happen. "Either," he writes, "the existence of the same passion or interest in a majority at the same time must be prevented, or the majority, having such coexistent passion or interest," as he puts it, "must be rendered, by their number and local situation, unable to concert and carry into effect schemes of oppression." Now in order for either or both of these effects to happen, we must, Hamilton says, "emphatically avoid setting up" what he calls a "[pure democracy] by which I mean," Madison writes, "a society consisting of a small number of citizens, who assemble and administer the government in person"—for, in such a pure democratic society, the assembled majority has direct political power and will easily coalesce into a unified faction. Some degree of mob rule, guided by demagogues, is the all-too-common fate of direct democracies.

Madison is here contradicting a basic premise of the whole Anti-Federalist, classically inspired republican vision. Madison is denying that participatory democracies or republics where the homogeneous majority has direct control over the government foster republican liberty. Madison is insisting that all the historical evidence shows, to the contrary, that such democracies endanger the liberty of individuals and minorities through the tyranny of the majority as a faction.

What we must set up, he says, instead of democracy in the classic sense, is what he calls a "[republic] by which I mean," he writes, "a government in which the scheme of representation takes place." Madison goes on to define exactly what the difference is between democracy and a republic, such as the constitution is establishing, and he does so in the following very careful formulation:

> The two great points of difference, [he writes] between a democracy and a republic, are, first, the delegation of the government, in the latter [that is, the republic] to a small number of citizens elected by the rest; secondly, [he says] the greater number of citizens, and the

greater sphere of country, over which the latter [that is, the republic] may be extended.

Here we see the real heart of this new Madisonian republican vision. The new American constitution aims not at a confederacy of small democratic participatory republics, but instead at one large extended mass republic, where the people never can assemble to govern directly and, hence, where the majority can never unite and become directly oppressive of minorities and individuals. But the most important consideration in this regard is not simply that the country's territory and numbers will be too big for the majority ever to physically assemble in one place; more important is the fact that the majority will be so diverse and so riven by conflicting factional interests trying to oppress one another, especially economic, that it will rarely share the same interests or, when it does, it will have great difficulty in becoming aware of that sharing.

As Madison puts it in his most important single statement explaining what, as he puts it, "... principally [is to] ... render factious combinations less to be dreaded." He writes:

> Extend the sphere, and you take in a greater variety of parties and interests; you make it less probable that a majority of the whole will have a common motive to invade the rights of other citizens; or, if such a common motive exists, it will be more difficult for all who feel it to discover their own strength, and to act in unison with each other. ... Hence, [he goes on to say] it clearly appears that the same advantage which a republic has over a democracy, in controlling the effects of faction, is enjoyed by a large over a small republic ... is enjoyed by the union over the states composing it. The influence of factious leaders may kindle a flame within their particular states, but it will be unable to spread a general conflagration through the other states: a religious sect [he says] may degenerate into a political faction in a part of the confederacy; but the variety of sects dispersed over the entire face of it must secure the national councils against any danger from that source: a rage for paper money, for an abolition of debts, for an equal division of property or for any other improper or wicked project, will be less apt to pervade the whole body of the union, than a particular member of it; in the same proportion as such a malady is more likely to taint a particular county or district, than an entire state.

Madison, in effect, stands the Anti-Federalist argument on its head in at least two major respects. In the first place, where the Anti-Federalists follow classical republican theory in seeking homogeneity of the populace and deplore a situation where, as recall "Brutus" lamented, "there will be a constant clashing of opinions; and the representatives of one part will be continually striving against those of the other." It's precisely that such "clashing," such striving against one another that Madison is saying is the key to maintaining liberty in a republic. That, of course, is very hard for the Anti-Federalists to accept. As the writer who calls himself "Centinel" writes, in his first letter, "If the administrators of every government are actuated by views of private interest and ambition, how is the welfare and happiness of the community to be the result of such jarring adverse interests?"

In the second place, Madison has a fundamentally opposed conception of how representation should work. Where the Anti-Federalists worry about the distancing of representatives from the people and from the people's control, including worrying about the fact that each represents a vast number of constituents whom he cannot possibly know well or resemble and mirror, it is just such removal of the representative from his constituents, it is just such representation of large diverse constituencies that Madison sees as the keys to safe as well as effective representative government. Because if the representatives are rather few in number, each representing a large populous district, it's more likely that each will have to win election by appealing to a broader coalition of competing and compromising factions in his district. It's much more likely that he'll represent a unified majority. If the representatives are, after being elected, fairly independent of the voters for a period of time, it's more likely when they meet in the government with other representations, that they will seek, among themselves, compromises and shifting coalitions and broker deals, which will have the effect that law and policy will take into account the welfare of much broader portions of the populace.

In the next lecture, we will deepen and broaden our understanding of the contrast between Madison's republican vision and that of his Anti-Federalist opponents.

# Lecture Eight
# The Argument over Representation

**Scope:**  The next great question is: How are the powers of the representatives to be distributed in this new republican vision so as to make the central government energetic, stable, and not a threat to republican freedom? "Publius" shows the degree to which he agrees with the Anti-Federalists that the most powerful part of a truly republican government must be the law-making body that is both directly dependent on, and sympathetic with, the people. Madison argues—against the Anti-Federalists—that the proposed House of Representatives does adequately meet this criterion, and it is in the debate over the adequacy of the proposed House that the contrasts between the competing conceptions of representation become most concrete and clear.

# Outline

I.  There is a deep contrast between the new Madisonian republican vision and that of the more classically oriented Anti-Federalists.

  A.  The Anti-Federalists are still concerned with trying to repress the spirit of faction from becoming prevalent in the citizenry while the Madisonian vision not only accepts faction but makes it an animating spirit of the republic.

  B.  The Anti-Federalists, following the classical principles, want to keep the reins of government more directly in the hands of the people, but for Madison such a removal is the one key to safe and effective representative government.

  1.  Madison states that the new constitution aims at the unclassical goal of excluding the people from any direct role in their government.

  2.  Unlike in classical democracies and republics, the American citizenry will be only indirectly engaged in the politics and governance of its society.

II.  It might at first appear that Madison's republican vision is based on the assumption that virtue can be dispensed with or replaced by the checking and balancing of the competitive struggle of competing selfish economic interest groups; this impression, however, is incomplete and we must look at the higher ingredient in Madison's republican vision.

A. In *Federalist* 10, Madison argues for the new conception of representative government removed from the populace.
   1. He praises such representative government not only for its ability to channel the selfish interest group struggle but also because it has a crucial elevating effect by putting the levers of governmental power in the hands of a tiny minority of representatives elected by the rest.
   2. Madison continues to count on virtue but only as found in a tiny minority.

B. Hamilton, in *Federalist* 35 and 36, argues that the character of the representative elite expected in the new American system is rather unclassical.
   1. The new elite will be dominated by the "members of the learned professionals" (e.g., lawyers).
   2. The virtuous in the new republican vision are expected to be more sympathetic to commerce and commercialism than the members of the elite as envisaged in classical republicanism.

C. We see, as regards the concern for virtue, another way in which the Madisonian vision runs counter to the Anti-Federalist vision.
   1. When the Anti-Federalists speak of the virtue that a republic needs, they do so in the spirit of Montesquieu.
   2. When the Anti-Federalists speak of elected representatives, they tend to express distrust and fear of their likely corruption.
   3. Madison, in contrast, distrusts and fears more potentially oppressive tendencies in the people.

D. Thomas Jefferson objected to this Madisonian outlook.
   1. Is it reasonable to expect that the people will be good electors if they do not themselves have a substantial portion of civic virtue?
   2. Can the people be expected to develop real civic virtue if they are not required to engage in direct political experience?
   3. Is not decentralization of government through powerful state and local governments essential to the civic education of the populace?
   4. What does the Federalist vision contain that promotes or cultivates these qualities among the people?

**E.** The Federalists argue that the best way to foster civic virtue is by creating a central government.

    **1.** The institutions of the central government will insure an administration that is just, effective, and has the power to influence state and local government.

    **2.** *That*, the Federalists submit, is what will best inspire, in talented individuals, a vocation for public service and draw them to public life, instilling in the most talented a noble ambition to take part in the government.

**III.** The next major dimension of the Federalist republican vision is the structuring of institutions that will channel the representatives so as to make powers both effective and checked and balanced from within.

    **A.** In *Federalist* 37, Madison stresses that the combining of these two goals was difficult for the Constitutional Convention.

        **1.** A big source of the difficulty was what Madison labels the "erroneous principles" of all classically inspired republican confederations.

        **2.** Madison insists in Paper 39 that it is sufficient for a republic to be "a government which derives all its powers directly or indirectly from the great body of the people; and is administered by persons holding their offices during pleasure, for a limited period, or during good behaviour."

    **B.** Madison agrees with the Anti-Federalists that the most powerful part of a truly republican government must be the law-making body but argues against the Anti-Federalists that the proposed House of Representatives adequately meets these criteria.

**IV.** It is in the debate over the adequacy of the proposed House that the similarities and contrasts between the competing conceptions of representation become most clear.

    **A.** Regarding the length of the term of office, Madison further agrees with the Anti-Federalists that "frequent elections are unquestionably the only policy, by which this dependence and sympathy can be effectually secured."

        **1.** He disputes the Anti-Federalist insistence that annual elections are required.

        **2.** The Anti-Federalists complain that the House's biennial elections make representatives too little dependent on constituents.

3. Madison insists that biennial elections are not different from annual elections and adds that two years is a minimal period needed to allow the representatives sufficient time to acquire the knowledge necessary to do their jobs.

**B.** The more profound disagreement emerges over the question of the number of representatives and the proportion between each representative and the number of his constituents.
　　1. The Anti-Federalists complain that the House should be much larger, with a much smaller number of constituents for each member.
　　2. Madison points out that with the future growth of the American population, within only 25 years the House will contain several hundred members—which will make it less likely for the House to coalesce into a unified elite.
　　3. Madison also points out that in a large House the assembly would begin to take on the qualities of a mob and be more likely to produce the oligarchic tendencies about which the Anti-Federalists worry.
　　4. Madison argues in Paper 56 that it is not important that the members of the national legislature be intimately familiar with all local matters.
　　5. Madison strongly reasserts the propriety of striving for representatives who do not resemble their constituents but are instead distinguished by their virtues.

**C.** Madison deplores "the indiscriminate and unbounded jealousy" that the Anti-Federalists evince for anyone elected to a position of national power.
　　1. In Paper 57, Madison criticizes the Anti-Federalists for having too little faith in the virtue of the people.
　　2. The Anti-Federalists' great concern for virtue in the citizenry is mixed with a great worry about that virtue's fragility.
　　3. It is the Madisonian republican vision, rather than the Anti-Federalist vision, that is arguably closer to the classical republican tradition in respect to the need for relying, in some measure, on a free people's demand and respect for virtue in its leaders.

**Essential Reading:**

"Cato," Fifth Letter; in Storing, *The Complete Anti-Federalist*, Vol. 2, pp. 116–19.

"The Federal Farmer," 12th letter; in Storing, *The Complete Anti-Federalist*, Vol. 2, pp. 294–301.

*The Federalist*, Papers 52–58 and 63 (review Papers 9, 10, 35, and 36).

**Supplementary Reading:**

Epstein, *The Political Theory of The Federalist*, Chapter 9.

Storing, *What the Anti-Federalists Were For*, Chapter 6.

**Questions to Consider:**

1. To what extent do you find Madison's responses to the Anti-Federalist critiques of the House of Representatives adequate, and to what extent inadequate?

2. Which of the two sides' understandings of the role of virtue in republican life do you find more persuasive and why?

# Lecture Eight—Transcript
## The Argument over Representation

At the end of the last lecture, we began to appreciate the full meaning of the deep contrast between the new Madisonian republican vision and that of the more classically oriented Anti-Federalists. One fundamental contrast is that the Anti-Federalists, following the principles of classical republicanism, are still concerned to try to prevent or repress the spirit of faction from becoming prevalent in the citizenry. The Anti-Federalists are still guided by the ideal of a homogeneous and harmonious or even fraternal citizenry. While the new Madisonian vision not only accepts faction, but makes the spirit of faction an animating spirit of the republic.

Another basic contrast is that the Anti-Federalists, following the classical principles, want to keep the reins of government more directly in the hands of the people. So, they worry about the distancing of representatives from the people and from the people's control. But for Madison, it's just such removal of the representatives from their constituents that is one key to safe as well as effective representative government.

Madison later states even more emphatically and explicitly that the new constitution aims at the unclassical goal of excluding the people, as a whole, from any direct role in their government. In Paper 63 he says that while the classical republics were not totally unfamiliar with some version of representation, "the true distinction," he writes, between the classical democracy and the new American republic lies—and this he puts in italics—"*in the total exclusion of the people, in their collective capacity, from any share in* [the government]." Unlike the citizens of classical democracies and republics, the American citizenry will be only indirectly engaged in the politics and governance of their society. To a much greater degree than in the classical republic, the American people will be absorbed in their private, factional, economic pursuits. They will become politically engaged chiefly in order to protect those factional pursuits, and the private liberties they express.

At this point, it appears that Madison's republican vision is based on the assumption that virtue can be dispensed with or mostly replaced by the checking and balancing of the competitive struggle of economic, selfish interest groups, but this impression is very incomplete. It's too simple and one-sided and we must look now at the higher ingredient in Madison's republican vision.

For Madison has, in Paper 10, an additional argument for the new conception of representative government removed from the populace. He praises such representative government not only for its ability to channel the selfish interest group struggle. Representative government, he says, can first and foremost have a crucial elevating effect. By putting the levers of power in the hands of a tiny minority of representatives, elected by the rest, the effect will be, Madison writes:

> To refine and enlarge the public views, by passing them through the medium of a chosen body of citizens, whose wisdom may best discern the true interest of their country, and whose patriotism and love of justice will be least likely to sacrifice it [that is, the true interest of the country] to temporary or partial considerations. Under such a regulation, [he writes] it may well happen that the public voice, pronounced by the representatives of the people, will be more consonant to the public good than if pronounced by the people themselves, convened for the purpose.

From this we see that Madison does continue to count on virtue, on wisdom, on patriotism, on love of justice, as he says, but as found in the few, in a tiny minority, elected by the rest. Madison reveals here that his new republicanism does not altogether break with the classical republican tradition in its original, aristocratic dimension, as opposed to its Montesquieuan, more democratic convention.

Madison even indicates here that his new republican vision hopes to succeed better at achieving some measure of that classical aristocratic aspiration than the classical republics themselves ever did in practice, but we must immediately note that Hamilton, in the subsequent Papers 35 and 36, explains more concretely that the character of the representative elite expected in this new American system is rather unclassical. The new elite that the American system expects will be dominated by what Hamilton calls "the members of the learned professions"—which is a flattering term for what he means, namely, lawyers—who he expects, he says, to, as he puts it, "feel a neutrality to the rivalships among the different branches of industry," and "be likely to prove an impartial arbiter between them."

The virtuous are not so much expected, as they were in the classical republican vision, to be found among the farmers, great and small. The virtuous in this new republican vision are expected to be much more sympathetic to commerce and to commercialism, to money-making, to material acquisitiveness, than were the members of the elite as envisaged in classical republicanism.

We see here, as regards to the concern for virtue, another way in which the Madisonian vision runs directly counter to the Anti-Federalist vision. When the Anti-Federalists speak of the virtue that a republic needs, they do so in a more Montesquieuan spirit. They think chiefly of virtue in the populace, in the mass of the citizens who do not hold office, in the electors rather than the elected. When the Anti-Federalists speak of the elected representatives in terms of their virtue and vice, they tend to express distrust and fear, of the likely corruption of the elected representatives. The Anti-Federalists harp on the overweening ambition, and the greed, that's likely to develop in those who attain positions of great governmental power, especially when those who are elected are not farmers and are not tied to the management of their own farms. This is one major reason why the Anti-Federalists want to cultivate vigorous and vigilant civic virtue in the people, who they hope will remain rooted in agrarian independence so that the people will guard against the corrupting and oligarchic tendencies in their elected representative elites.

Madison, by contrast, distrusts and fears more the potentially oppressive tendencies in the people, coalescing in majoritarian faction. Madison and the Federalists hope that the rare virtues of some of the elected representatives, and by no means only farmers, will play a role in checking the people's majoritarian tyrannical tendencies. It's possible to articulate here a rather powerful objection to this Madisonian outlook, an objection that was made by Madison's friend Thomas Jefferson:

> Is it reasonable [Jefferson asks] to expect that the people will be good electors, that is, able and inclined to appreciate and to vote for statesmen, and not apt to be seduced by demagogues, if the people do not themselves have a substantial portion of civic virtue? And can the people be expected to develop real civic virtue, if the people are not required and called upon to engage in more direct political experience, as well as having the economic stability and independence that comes with the ownership of a farm? Is not decentralization of government, providing powerful state and local governments, essential to civic education of the populace? [Jefferson asked.]

What, the Anti-Federalists ask, does the Federalist vision contain in it that promotes or cultivates these qualities amongst the people? Is it not a grave weakness of the Federalist vision that it takes virtue too much for granted, in both populace and leaders? It's hard to deny that the Federalists do seem, in some measure, vulnerable to this criticism; thus we hear Madison saying, in Paper 55:

> As there is a degree of depravity in mankind which requires a certain degree of circumspection and distrust, so there are other qualities in human nature which justify a certain portion of esteem and confidence. Republican government [he says] presupposes the existence of these qualities in a higher degree than any other form.

But is it enough to merely "presuppose" virtue? Can it be presupposed?

Now, the Federalists can reply to this challenge that they do not simply take for granted some degree of civic virtue in leaders and in citizens. The Federalists do also suggest and argue that their republicanism actually does a better job of cultivating civic virtue. How so? Well, they argue, the best way in practice to foster civic virtue is by creating a central government whose institutions ensure an administration that's fair, or just, and vigorously effective, and which has the power to influence the state and local levels of government so that they must follow this fine model of effectiveness and fairness. *That*, the Federalists insist and submit, is what will best inspire, in talented individuals all over the country, a vocation for public service. That's what will draw the best to public life, instilling in the most talented and noble ambition to take part in such a fine government. That's what will arouse in the populace a respect and an appreciation for such public-spirited representatives, along with a respect for the law and for the constitutional order, all of which will amount to a popular spirit of sober patriotism, grounded in the enlightened self-interest of individuals who see with gratitude that their prosperity, their economic interest, are dependent on the proper functioning of their constitutional institutions.

This brings us to the next major dimension of the Federalist republican vision. What we've now seen, the new idea of an extended, faction-ridden republic, administered by a tiny number of pretty removed representatives—that's all the foundation, but only the foundation. What must be built, now, on this foundation, is a structure of institutions that will channel the representatives, in the exercise of their powers, so as to make those powers both energetically effective as well as stable and checked and balanced from within.

In Paper 37 Madison begins the transition to this theme by stressing that the combining of these two distinct goals—that is, stable energy and protection for republican liberty—was a very great difficulty for the Constitutional Convention. A big source of the difficulty was what Madison labels, the "erroneous principles" of all earlier, classically inspired republican confederations. Because according to that traditional way of thinking, as Madison puts it:

> The genius of republican liberty, appears or seems to demand ... not only that all power should be derived from the people; but, that those entrusted with it should be kept in dependence on the people, by a short duration of their appointments; and that, even during this short period, the trust should be placed not in a few, but in a number of hands.

Against this, Madison insists in Paper 39 that it is "sufficient" for a republic, that it be, as he puts it, "a government which derives all its powers directly or indirectly from the great body of the people; and is administered by persons holding their offices during pleasure, for a limited period, or during good behaviour."

Still, when Madison turns to the design of the Federal government, he shows in the series of papers in which he discusses the proposed House of Representatives, Papers 52 through 58, that he agrees with the Anti-Federalists, that the most powerful part of a truly republican government must be the law-making body, which must be directly dependent on the people and also intimately sympathetic with the people. As Madison puts it in Paper 52, "it is essential to liberty ... that the [legislative] branch ... should have an immediate dependence on, and an intimate sympathy with, the people." Madison, of course, argues against the Anti-Federalists that the proposed House of Representatives does adequately meet these criteria.

It's in the debate over the adequacy of the proposed House of Representatives that the precise similarities and contrasts between these competing conceptions of representation held by the Federalists and the Anti-Federalists become most concrete and clear. In the first place, they argue over the length of term of office. And as regards that, Madison goes on at once to make clear that he agrees further with the Anti-Federalists that, as he says, "Frequent elections are unquestionably the only policy, by which this dependence and sympathy can be effectually secured."

Madison disputes the repeated Anti-Federalist insistence, which "Cato" had stressed on the authority of Montesquieu and as we saw in an earlier reading, there is stressed that annual elections are required. No, Madison insists, annual elections are not necessary. The Anti-Federalists repeatedly complain about the House of Representatives, that its biennial elections make it such that the Representatives are too little dependent on their constituents. Annual elections are needed, the Anti-Federalists argue, to make the representatives truly dependent on the voters and to keep them in sympathy with them. In the words of the Massachusetts writer who signs himself "John DeWitt," "[If] the elections would be annual, the persons elected would reside in the center of you, their interests would be yours, they would be subject to your immediate control." He goes on to complain, in this proposed House of Representatives, he says, "… they are chosen for double the time, during which, however well disposed, they become strangers to the very people choosing them, they reside at a distance from you, you have no control over them, you cannot observe their conduct."

Madison replies by insisting that biennial elections are not as different in these effects from annual elections as is claimed. He adds that there is a great advantage of biennial over annual elections, namely that two years is a minimal period needed to allow the representatives sufficient time to acquire the knowledge that's necessary to do their jobs adequately. Knowledge that, as Madison puts it in Paper 53, "… can only be attained, or at least thoroughly attained, by actual experience in the station which requires the use of it." Madison does have to admit that in most of the states, after the Revolution and in the national Congress, under the Articles of Confederation, the term for the legislators is set at one year or less. But Madison argues that since the scope of the power and responsibility of the new national legislature is going to be much greater than that of either the state legislatures or the existing Congress, the business will be much more complex and difficult to learn.

A more profound disagreement emerges in regards to the question of the number of representatives and the proportion between each representative and the number of his constituents. Over and over again the Anti-Federalists complain, on the basis of their conception of representation as properly resembling the constituents, as knowing and being known by living among the constituents, that the House should be much larger, with a much smaller number of constituents electing each member. Thus, "The Federal Farmer" protests in his third letter, "I have no idea," he says, how it's conceivable that "the interests, feelings, and opinions [of] millions of people, especially touching internal taxation, can be collected in such a house," as is being designed in this constitution, in which each delegate, he points out, is supposed to represent at least fifty thousand constituents. As he says in his second letter:

A full and equal representation is that which possesses the same interests, feelings, opinions, and views the people themselves would, were they all assembled. A fair representation, therefore, should be so regulated, that every order of men in the community, according to the common course of elections, can have a share in it, in order to allow professional men, merchants, traders, farmers, mechanics, etc. to bring a just proportion of their best informed men respectively into the legislature, the representation must be considerably numerous.

In his 12th letter, "The Federal Farmer" proposes an alternative conception of the House of Representatives. This is fascinating because it is one of the places where the Anti-Federalists give a concrete alternative for a specific institution. He puts it this way:

I see no way [he writes] to fix elections on a proper footing, and to render tolerably equal and secure the federal representation, but by increasing the representation, so as to have one representative for each district in which the electors may conveniently meet in one place, and at one time, and choose by a majority. Perhaps this might be affected pretty generally, by fixing one representative for each twelve thousand inhabitants. ... By thus increasing the representation [he writes] ... we fix what, in my mind, is of far more importance than brilliant talents, I mean a sameness, as to residence and interests, between the representative and his constituents.

Madison has to admit some merit in this worry of the Anti-Federalists. In Paper 55, Madison acknowledges what he calls "the weight of character, and the apparent force of argument," of those who have advanced this criticism. That, as he puts it, "... so small a number of representatives will ... not possess a proper knowledge of the local circumstances of their numerous constituents [and] that they'll be taken from that class of citizens which will sympathize least with the feelings of the mass of the people, and be most likely to aim at a permanent elevation of the few."

Back in the Paper 10, Madison had acknowledged the danger that, as he put it there, "By enlarging too much the number of electors, you render the representative too little acquainted with all their local circumstances and lesser interests." But he had characteristically added the danger on the other side. He wrote, "... by reducing it," that is, the number of voters, "too much, you render [the representative] unduly attached to these, and too little fit to comprehend and pursue great and national objects."

Madison continued by saying, "The federal constitution forms a happy combination in this respect." Here in Paper 55, talking about the House of Representatives, Madison explains this "happy combination" more fully, by first pointing out that, with the future growth in America's projected population, we can predict, Madison says, that within only 25 years the House will contain several hundred members, which will make it less likely that it will coalesce into a tiny unified oppressive elite, as the Anti-Federalists fear.

Then in the second place, Madison begins to point out that there are grave problems involved in having a House of Representatives composed of a much larger number than just a few hundred, because then the House, itself, would begin to take on the qualities of a mob, such as is always seen in large assemblies and such as blighted the civic life of ancient democracies like the Athenian. In one of his most eloquent sentences, Madison writes, "In all very numerous assemblies, of whatever characters composed, passion never fails to wrest the scepter from reason. Had every Athenian citizen been a Socrates, every Athenian assembly would still have been a mob."

The mob characteristic of a very large House of Representatives would by no means be dangerous only because it would signal an impassioned excess of majority rule. Paradoxically, Madison argues, a very large House would be more likely to produce precisely the oligarchic tendencies that the Anti-Federalists are so worried about. Because in Paper 58 Madison points out, in a large House you're likely to get the prevalence of demagogues within the House. Again, Madison appeals here to the classical republican experience—but again, as something to be avoided, rather than as something to be followed.

> In all legislative assemblies [Madison writes] the greater the number composing them may be, the fewer will be the men who will in fact [actually] direct the proceedings. [For, he goes on to say:] The larger the number, the greater will be the proportion of members of limited information and of weak capacities. Now, [he says] it is precisely on characters of this description that the eloquence and address of the few are known to act with all their force. In the ancient republics, [he says] where the whole body of the people assembled in person, a single orator, or an artful statesman, was generally seen to rule with as complete a sway as if a scepter had been placed in his single hand. On

> the same principle, [Madison goes on] the more multitudinous a representative assembly may be rendered, the more it will partake of the infirmities incident to collective meetings of the people. ... The countenance of the government may become more democratic, but the soul that animates it will be more oligarchic.

Then in the third place, Madison argues in Paper 56, that it is not as important as the Anti-Federalists' claim that the members of the national legislature be intimately familiar with all local matters. Because what the national legislature will deal with is mainly matters that concern the whole country, matters that all or many localities have in common. So the analogy with the knowledge required of a state legislator, he argues, is somewhat misleading.

Then last, but by no means least, Madison strongly reasserts the propriety of striving and hoping to have representatives who do not resemble their constituents in being merely typical or average people, but instead persons who are distinguished by their virtues and therefore to be given more trust than the Anti-Federalists allow.

Madison deplores what he calls at the end of Paper 55, "the indiscriminate and unbounded jealousy" that the Anti-Federalists seem to evince for anyone who is elected to a position of national power.

> The sincere friends of liberty, [Madison writes] who give themselves up to the extravagancies of this passion, [that is, this jealousy about elites] are not aware of the injury they do their own cause ... Were the pictures [he writes] which have been drawn by the political jealousy of some among us, faithful likenesses of the human character, the inference would be, that there is not sufficient virtue among men for self-government.

Paradoxically, in Paper 57, Madison criticizes the Anti-Federalists for having too little faith in the virtue; not only the virtue of the representatives, but also the virtue of the people, who will be doing the electing freely and can be counted on, Madison insists, to chose their representatives with some judgment as to who among the candidates possesses most virtue and wisdom. After all, Madison writes, "Who are to be the objects of popular choice?" He answers:

> Every citizen whose merit may recommend him to the esteem and confidence of his country. No qualification of wealth, of birth, of religious faith, or of civil profession, is permitted to fetter the

judgment, or disappoint the inclination of the people. ... And if it be asked, [he goes on] what is to restrain the House of Representatives from making legal discriminations in favor of themselves, and a particular class of the society? Well, I answer, [Madison says] above all, the vigilant and manly spirit which actuates the people of America; a spirit which nourishes freedom, and in return is nourished by it.

If we look back to the Anti-Federalists on this major point, to see how they view the electorate's respect and demand for virtue in its elected leaders, we see that, paradoxically, the Anti-Federalists, in their great concern for virtue in the citizenry, mixed that with a great worry about that virtue's fragility or dissipation. They worry about the ease with which the people can be duped by the clever few. As John Francis Mercer puts it, "The aristocracy, who move by system and design, and always under the colorable pretext of securing property, ... has ever proved an overmatch for the multitude, who never act but from their feelings, and are never permitted to feel *until it is too late*." Here, once again, we see that it's the Madisonian republican vision, rather than the Anti-Federalist, that is arguably closer to the classical republican tradition in this key respect; that is, in respect to the need for relying, in some measure, on a free people's demand and respect for virtue in its leaders.

The Anti-Federalists attack the design of the proposed House of Representatives not only because they think it's likely to become corrupted from within, they also attack its design because they see it as being, in relation to the other, less popular branches of government—the Senate, and President, and even the Supreme Court—too weak. They predict that the House will be overpowered and corrupted from outside, as well as from within. They predict that it's going to be dominated by the more powerful and much more elitist Senate and Presidency and Supreme Court.

This introduces us to the debate over the meaning of separation of powers, and checks and balances, within the federal structure, which will be the focus of the next lecture.

# Lecture Nine
# Disputing Separation of Powers, Part 1

**Scope:** The Anti-Federalists worry that the popularly elected House of Representatives will tend to be too weak in relation to the other great institutions of the federal government. Madison counters with the argument that, in a democracy, the power that is naturally greatest and most likely to conceive of itself as entitled to dominate is that of the legislative body that directly represents the people. This concern animates the proposed constitution's conception of how the powers of government should be separated so as to check and balance one another. The Anti-Federalists charge that the constitution flagrantly violates the doctrine of strict separation among the legislative, executive, and judicial powers of government—and does so most dangerously in the creation of the aristocratic Senate. Madison rejoins that this shows a failure to grasp the central idea of the doctrine: that government should be checked by an internally conflicting interaction involving considerable overlap among its distinct powers. The fulcrum of the system, in Madison's eyes, is a Senate that is not elected directly and that is intended as an assembly of elder statesmen.

## Outline

I.   The Anti-Federalists attack the proposed House of Representatives not only because they think it likely to become corrupted from within but also because in relation to the Senate, the Presidency, and the Supreme Court, it is too weak.

   A.   The Anti-Federalists fear that the House will be overpowered by the less popular branches of government.

   B.   To this fear, Madison points out that the House is explicitly given the originating power over all expenditure of money and that, in a republic, it will be the governmental institution that most directly represents the people that will have the most political clout.

   C.   It is precisely this power that worries Madison and Hamilton.
      1.   The House, in the eyes of the Federalists, is the most dangerous part of the national government and most in need of being checked and balanced.

2. This danger arises because the House genuinely represents the will of the people on account of its reasonably frequent elections and its being numerous enough to reflect the country's diversity.

3. If the people are wise, they will adopt and support a constitutional order in which even the institution that most directly represents their majority will at any time be checked and balanced by institutions that stand on a competing basis.

D. In response to the Anti-Federalists' worry about the weakness of the popular branch of legislature, the Federalists retort that this is exactly opposite to what one should worry about in designing a republican constitution.

II. It is time for us to turn to the argument between the two sides over the meaning of the separation of powers and whether or not the proposed constitution embodies an adequate separation and balance of powers.

A. Madison opens his discussion by acknowledging that the Anti-Federalists have lodged as one of their "principle objections" the charge that the proposed constitution flagrantly violates the separation of powers.

1. This is the great principle taught by Montesquieu, that the three basic functions of government must be kept in separate hands.

2. The Anti-Federalists decry the way the proposed constitution institutes overlap and the sharing of power among the institutions that should be more exclusively legislative, executive, or judicial.

B. Madison responds by going back to the philosophical and theoretical basis of the separation of powers.

1. Madison insists that there has to be considerable overlapping and sharing if the separation is to accomplish its purpose.

2. The purpose is not only to limit the power of the government by dividing its three component functions into separate branches but also to make the power of each branch be checked by the other two as the three work together.

3. Madison elaborates that the intended checking and balancing cannot take place unless "these departments be so far connected and blended, as to give to each a constitutional control over the others."

C. The three powers of government are going to need to cooperate while competing; thus, each of the three branches needs the leverage of having some control over each of the other two rival branches.

D. What the Anti-Federalists do not appreciate, Madison and Hamilton suggest, is the degree to which the proposed constitution makes it safe to give enormous power to the central government by structuring the central government in such a way that it is checked and balanced from within.

III. Because, in a republic, the elected legislative branch is most likely to tend to dominate over the executive and judiciary, it is essential that the legislative branch be itself split into two competing houses with different sources of authority.

A. The most active struggle is designed to take place among the three institutions that make up two of the three branches: the legislative and the executive.
   1. These, unlike the judiciary, are the branches that do most of the work of governing.
   2. These are the branches that are, in different ways, responsible to the people.

B. Hamilton stresses in Paper 60 that in order to ensure real competitive diversity among the House, Senate, and Presidency, each needs to be selected on very different bases.
   1. Only the House is to be elected directly by the people.
   2. The President is to be chosen by an elite electoral college made up of delegates elected by the people in each state.
   3. Senators are to be appointed or elected by the state legislatures.

IV. It is important at this point to spotlight the special role that the Senate is designed to have in the proposed system.

A. In Madison's conception, the Senate is the linchpin of the constitutional system of separation of powers.

B. Papers 62–66 show that the Senate is intended not only to constrain the House's tendency toward overweening power but also to counteract some likely defective tendencies and qualifications of the House.

1. The Federalists see the House as becoming, with the growth of the United States, a body of legislators numbering in the hundreds, which will make meetings more subject to the passions of a crowd.
2. The members of the House are likely to be people without much prior experience in government and with rather narrow views.
3. The Senate is to be a much smaller assembly, unlikely to take on the characteristics of a mob.
4. Senators are expected to be elder, experienced legislators.
5. Senators represent entire states and thus a much broader constituency.
6. Senators will serve for longer terms, with a strong likelihood of being reelected.

**C.** Not only are senators expected to be individuals with superior qualifications but their collective answerability is also to be much greater than that of members of the House.

**D.** Madison shows in Paper 63 that he expects the Senate will be independent enough of the people to be able to check and balance not only the House but even the people as a whole.

## Essential Reading:

"Centinel" [Samuel Bryan], First Letter; in Storing, *The Complete Anti-Federalist*, Vol. 2, pp. 136–43.

"Cincinnatus" [perhaps Arthur Lee, the brother of Richard Henry Lee], Fourth Essay; in Storing, *The Complete Anti-Federalist*, Vol. 6, pp. 17–22.

"The Federal Farmer," 11th Letter; in Storing, *The Complete Anti-Federalist*, Vol. 2, pp. 286–94.

*The Federalist*, Papers 47–48, 51, 62–66.

Mason, "Objections to the Constitution of Government formed by the Convention" in Storing, *The Complete Anti-Federalist*, Vol. 2, pp. 11–13.

Montesquieu, *The Spirit of the Laws*, Book 11, Chapter 6.

## Supplementary Reading:

Storing, *What the Anti-Federalists Were For*, Chapter 7.

D. and S. Wirls, *The Invention of the United States Senate*, Chapter 6.

**Questions to Consider:**

1.  To what extent does our contemporary Senate bear out the predictions of each side about what the Senate would be like in its character and functioning?

2.  Considering the House of Representatives as it exists today, in what respects do you find each side's predictions about the character of the House of Representatives to be valid or invalid?

# Lecture Nine—Transcript
## Disputing Separation of Powers, Part 1

We've now seen that the cornerstone of the new constitutional structure is the proposed House of Representatives. This is the part of the federal government that will most directly embody the represented will of the people. This is the most democratic part of the structure.

In the last lecture, we saw how Madison rebuts Anti-Federalist complaints that the design of the proposed House is deeply flawed. But the Anti-Federalists attack the proposed House of Representatives not only because they think it likely to become corrupted from within. They also attack the proposed House as being, in relation to the less popular branches of government, the Senate and President and even the Supreme Court, too weak. The Anti-Federalists fear that the House will be overshadowed, overpowered, and corrupted by the more powerful and even more elitist Senate and Presidency and Supreme Court.

To this fear, Madison's reply is twofold. First, he points out that the House is explicitly given the originating power over all expenditures of money. Article 1, Section 7 begins with the statement, "All bills for raising revenue shall originate in the House of Representatives." This means that not a dime can be spent by the government, for any reason, unless the authorization begins in the House, and, as Madison writes in Paper 58:

> This power over the purse may, in fact, be regarded as the most complete and effectual weapon with which any constitution can arm the immediate representatives of the people, for obtaining a redress of every grievance, and for carrying into effect every just and salutary measure.

Secondly, Madison argues that in a republic, where the people as a majority are the ultimate supreme moral and legitimate power, the source of all legitimacy, and where, in addition, the people through their militias are armed with the greatest military power, it will be the governmental institution that most directly represents the people which will wield by far the greatest moral authority, the greatest legitimacy. Hence, will tend to have the most political sway or clout.

Now it is precisely this power of the House that worries Madison and Hamilton. The House is, in the eyes of the Federalists, the most dangerous part of the national government, the institution most in need of being checked and balanced by other institutions. This danger arises despite or even because of some of the virtues Madison has argued are present in its design; above all, precisely because the House does genuinely represent the will of the people or of the majority of the people, on account of its reasonably frequent elections, and on account of being numerous enough to reflect adequately the diversity of the whole country.

These very virtues give to the House and its members a powerful temptation to assume that, since the House speaks for the majority of the people or is the delegated voice of the majority, it therefore embodies the deepest, long-term will of the people. On this basis, the Federalists warn, there will be a tendency in the House to steadily increase its power and eventually to dominate. But, if the people are wise, they will adopt and support a constitutional order in which no single institution can claim by itself to express the deepest, long-term will of the people. A wise people will adopt a system in which even or especially the institution that most directly represents their majority will at any time is checked and balanced by institutions that stand on a different, competing basis. As Hamilton says later, in Paper 71:

> The representatives of the people, in a popular assembly, seem sometimes to fancy that they are the people themselves, and betray strong symptoms of impatience and disgust at the least sign of opposition from any other quarter. ... And as they commonly have the people on their side, they always act with such momentum as to make it very difficult for the other members of the government to maintain the balance of the Constitution.

So it follows, as Madison writes in Paper 48, that, in his words:

> In a representative republic, where the executive magistracy is carefully limited ... and where the legislative power is exercised by an assembly, which is inspired, by a supposed influence over the people, with an intrepid confidence in its own strength ... it is against the enterprising ambition of this department that the people ought to indulge all their jealousy and exhaust all their precautions.

It's in response to the worry that the Anti-Federalists have about the popular branch of the legislature, that it's going to be too weak, that the Federalists retort that this is exactly opposite to what one should worry about in designing a republican constitution. The Federalists indicate that their worry about the potential threat from the excessive and domineering strength of the House of Representatives is based not only on theory, but on bitter experience. They point to what they have observed happening in many of the state governments, where there is an ominous tendency for the executive and judicial branches to be overpowered and dominated by the popularly elected Houses in the legislatures of the states.

The concern "Publius" has for limiting and checking this potentially dangerous power of the House of Representatives becomes most evident when we consider the papers framing those papers that are devoted to the House of Representatives, the papers that precede the ones on the House and the papers that follow. Because Madison defends and explains the House as the cornerstone of the proposed constitution's republicanism only after he has defended and explained in Papers 47 through 51 the constitution's commitment to a sound system of checks and balances, centered on the separation of powers.

It's time for us now to turn to these papers, and to the argument between the two sides, Federalists and Anti-Federalists, over the meaning of the separation of powers, and over whether or not the proposed constitution embodies an adequate separation and balance of powers.

Madison opens his discussion of the separation and balance of powers by acknowledging at the start of Paper 47 that those whom he calls, "the more respectable adversaries" have lodged as one of their "principle objections," as he puts it, the charge that the proposed constitution flagrantly violates the separation of powers. That is, the great set of principles taught by Montesquieu above all, that the three basic functions of government, first the lawmaking, then the law executing or administering, and then, finally, the judging, which applies the law in particular circumstances, must be kept in separate hands.

The Anti-Federalists decry the way the proposed constitution institutes all sorts of overlap and sharing of power among the institutions that should be kept separately and more exclusively either legislative, or executive, or judicial. They point out that the overlap and sharing is most obvious in the design of the executive, since to the President under this constitution is given a vast judicial power, through the right to pardon, and an enormous share in the legislative power, through the veto. But still worse, the Anti-Federalists point out, is the design of the Senate, the upper house of the legislative branch. Because the proposed Senate not only combines, with its proper legislative role, an awesome judicial role in that it sits as the court that tries impeachments, but much more dangerous, the Senate has what George Mason calls "an alarming Dependence and Connection [with] the supreme executive," on account of its participation, through its advice and consent, in making all treaties, and hence foreign policy, a strictly executive function. But still worse, the Anti-Federalists point out, the Senate has a share in the control over the appointments of major officers, both foreign and domestic, in the executive branch through its having to give its advice and consent to such appointments.

Madison responds to this Anti-Federalist alarm by saying, let's go back to the philosophical and theoretical basis of the separation of powers. To Montesquieu, who, as Madison says, is "the oracle who is always consulted and cited on this subject." Madison insists if we read carefully the famous passages in Book 11 of *The Spirit of the Laws* where Montesquieu lays out his teaching on the separation of powers, showing especially the way the separation of powers has emerged historically in the British Constitution and how it works to preserve the liberty for and of Englishmen, one sees, Madison insists, that when Montesquieu teaches that no two of the three distinct, fundamental functions should be placed in the same hands, he does not mean that there is to be no overlapping, no sharing at all of the three powers. On the contrary, Madison says, that betrays a complete misunderstanding of the doctrine. There has to be considerable overlapping and sharing, Madison insists, if the separation is to accomplish its purposes.

The purposes include not only the one that the Anti-Federalists focus on too exclusively, which is limiting the power of government overall by dividing its three component functions into separate branches. That's only part of the story, Madison says. The purpose is also and more importantly to make the divided powers capable of checking one another. Making so that each of the three branches is checked by the other two, as the three work together in a coordination that involves somewhat tense interaction, competition, and thus mutual limitation.

So it is a profound misunderstanding of this teaching, Madison argues in Paper 47, to think that Montesquieu means that the three departments, as Madison puts it, "ought to have ... no control over the acts of each other." On the contrary, as Madison goes on to elaborate in the Paper 48, the intended checking and balancing among the three cannot take place unless, in his words, "... these departments be so far connected and blended, as to give to each a constitutional control over the others [in order] to provide some practical security for each, against the invasion of the others."

Notice the way Madison uses the language of warfare, "invasion," and we'll see as we go on, he uses it more and more in this context. He's insisting that Montesquieu's teaching envisages a never-ending, interactive struggle, a kind of warfare, among the three powers. The idea is to bring into the heart of government, to instill among the parts of government, a version of that same intense competitiveness that is intended to characterize the society at large, where the competitive struggle among factions prevents the coalescence of any one overwhelming and potentially tyrannical majority faction and compels the building of shifting compromise coalitions among rivals in a tensely competitive cooperation.

The three powers of the national government are going to need to cooperate while competing, constantly, as rivals for power, resisting each other's tendency or temptation to try to dominate one another. Thus, each of the three branches needs the leverage of having some control over each of the other two rival branches. That means even some footholds in one another's domain. Thus for example, Madison says, a chief reason for the Presidential veto over legislation is to give the President a weapon that gives him defensive control over the legislative branch, to protect the executive power from becoming subordinated to the legislature. Thus the Senate, Madison says, is given the high judicial power of trying impeachments, as a way of giving the legislative branch defensive control over the judicial as well as the executive branch.

Eventually, in Paper 51, Madison steps back to lay out, synoptically, in one of the work's most famous and eloquent passages, the way in which the new American republicanism introduces endless conflict into what Madison calls the "interior structure of the government" itself.

> The great security [Madison writes] against a gradual concentration of the several powers in the same department, consists in giving to those who administer each department, the necessary constitutional means and personal motives, to resist encroachments of the others. The provision for defence must in this, as in all other cases, be made commensurate to the danger of attack. Ambition must be made to counteract ambition. The interest of the man must be connected with the constitutional rights of the place.

Then in a remarkable passage, Madison adds a kind of apology for this core competitive spirit of the whole constitutional system.

> It may be a reflection on human nature, [he says] that such devices should be necessary to control the abuses of government. But what is government itself, [he asks] but the greatest of all reflections on human nature? ... If angels were to govern men, neither external nor internal controls on government would be necessary. In

framing a government which is to be administered by men, over men, the great difficulty lies in this: you must first enable the government to control the governed; and in the next place oblige it to control itself. A dependence on the people is, no doubt, the primary control on the government ...

This, of course, is what the Anti-Federalists tend to rely on pretty exclusively. But it's not enough, Madison goes on to say. In his words:

> ... but experience has taught mankind the necessity of auxiliary precautions. This policy of supplying, by opposite and rival interests, the defect of better motives, might be traced through the whole system of human affairs, private as well as public. We see it particularly displayed in all the subordinate distributions of power; where the constant aim is, to divide and arrange the several offices in such a manner as that each may be a check on the other; that the private interest of every individual may be a sentinel over the public rights.

Notice that in these last words, Madison makes it clear that the aim is to bring that competitive, mutually checking, antagonistic spirit inside each of the three branches, and not only to promote the competition between the three branches.

What the Anti-Federalists are not sufficiently appreciating, Madison and Hamilton are now arguing, is the degree to which the proposed constitution makes it safe to give unlimited power to the central government, by structuring that government in such a way that it is checked and balanced from within, through the institution of a kind of permanent inner warfare among, and even within, each of the three branches. This is the Federalist answer to what we saw earlier was the great underlying Anti-Federalist question or challenge, namely, how can we safely do without a balancing equilibrium of power between the state and the national governments? Or what can we substitute for the power of the state governments to keep the central government under control?

Now, because in a republic, it is the elected legislative branch that is most likely to tend to dominate over the executive and the judiciary, it is essential that the legislative branch itself split into two competing houses, with very different bases of authority. As Madison puts it, since:

> In republican government, the legislative authority necessarily predominates, the remedy for this inconveniency is to divide the

legislature into different branches; and to render them, by different modes of election and different principles of action, as little connected with each other as the nature of their common functions and their common dependence on the society will admit.

We see now that the most active competitive struggle is designed to take place, not quite among the three branches of government, but rather, among the three institutions that make up two of those branches, the bicameral legislative and the executive. These, unlike the judiciary, are the branches that do most of the work of governing. These are, appropriately, the branches that are in different ways responsible to the people, answerable to the electorate for what they do. The judiciary is envisaged as being somewhat removed from the struggle, as being less active and less powerful.

Now as Hamilton stresses in Paper 60, in order to ensure real competitive diversity, avoid coalescence, among the House, Senate, and Presidency, they each need to be selected on three very different bases, arranged especially so as to counter the likely tendency to excessive power of the House of Representatives. As we've seen, in the Madisonian vision, it is crucial that, since the House embodies the most direct will of the people's majority, it needs to be balanced by bodies that are not so directly shaped by the popular majority. So only the House is to be elected directly by the people. The other two institutions are to be selected only indirectly by the people. The President is to be chosen by an elite electoral college made up of delegates elected by the people in each state. The plan is and was for these elected elite delegates to meet in secret, in each state, to deliberate among themselves and to give all the state's electoral votes to the person they decided on. The senators are also not to be elected directly by the people in each state.

Nowadays we tend to forget what a momentous departure is the direct election of the United States senators from the original intention of the founders. It was only in the early 20th century, in 1913, that the Constitution was amended, by the 17th Amendment, to have the senators directly elected by the people in each state. The original intention of the founders was a much less democratic base for the Senate. Senators were to be appointed by the state legislatures. As *The Federalist* explains, the assumption was that that would mean the senators would usually be state legislators themselves. In other words, the expectation was that the Senate would be made up largely of former state legislators or distinguished public figures, with a career behind them of experience in state legislatures or other civic service.

Senators would typically, it was expected, be men who had been recognized and honored through this elevation by their peers in the state legislatures.

As Hamilton says in Paper 27, "through the medium of the state legislatures, who are select bodies of men, and who are to appoint the members of the national Senate, there is reason to expect that this branch will generally be composed with peculiar care and judgment." So the Senate is thus envisaged as a relatively small assembly of elder experienced statesmen. If we step back and consider the electoral system as a whole, as it was intended originally, we can see that the intention of the original constitution is to create a procedure for electing the President and the Senate which very much mixes democratic with aristocratic process. As John Jay puts it in Paper 64:

> As the select assemblies for choosing the President, as well as the State legislatures who appoint the senators, will in general be composed of the most enlightened and respectable citizens, there is reason to presume that their attention and their votes will be directed to those men only who have become the most distinguished by their abilities and virtue.

We see here more concretely how the Federalists conceive of their new republic as embodying some substantial degree of the aristocratic ethos that characterized original classical republicanism and this practical ideal I spoke of earlier of the "mixed regime."

In this connection, it's appropriate at this point to spotlight the very special status and role that the Senate is designed to have in this proposed system. It's not too much of an exaggeration to say that, in Madison's conception, the Senate is the linchpin of the constitutional system of the separation of checks and balances. The Senate is that institution which, as Madison presents it, most clearly elevates and transforms the system, making the separation and balance of powers into something above and beyond a mere competition of predominantly selfish institutions and political actors. This special status and role of the Senate, and all that it implies, becomes clearer in the papers devoted to explaining and defending the Senate, numbers 62 through 66.

These papers show that the Senate is intended not only to constrain the House's tendency to overweening power, but also, as Madison stresses in Paper 62, to compensate for and to counteract what are expected to be some likely defective tendencies and qualifications of the House. Now, what are these specific dangers posed by the House of Representatives that the

Federalists design the Senate to remedy? In the first place, the Federalists see the House as soon becoming—after 20 or 30 more years with the growth of the U.S. population—a body numbering in the hundreds, which will make their meetings more subject to the passions of a crowd.

In the second place, the members of the House are likely, they think, to be often persons without much prior experience in government; businessmen, lawyers, people who have not served much and often people who aren't intending to spend many years in public service.

In the third place, the members of the House are likely to be persons of rather narrow views on account of the fact that they will be representing relatively smaller districts, with local and temporary perspectives, and also because they will be popularly elected by their local constituents for short terms of two years, and therefore will be more subject to the narrow and changing popular majoritarian passions in each of their districts.

What are the specific strengths which the Senate is supposed to have that compensate for these specific defects of the House? Well, first, the Senate is to be a much smaller assembly, two from each state, unlikely ever to take on the characteristics of a mob or crowd. Second, as we've already seen, the senators are expected to be elder, experienced legislators, selected and honored by their peers. As Madison puts it in Paper 62, "The nature of the senatorial trust, requiring greater extent of information and stability of character, requires, at the same time, that the senator should have reached a period of life most likely to supply these advantages."

In the third place, the senators represent entire states, and thus a much broader constituency. Fourth, the senators will serve for much longer terms, six years rather than two, with a strong likelihood of being reelected by their state legislatures or reappointed.

All of these characteristics will allow and encourage the senators to embrace a broader national perspective and to view things in the long term, which will be additionally encouraged, Madison argues, by the fact that they will have an international perspective, given the important role they're supposed to play by sharing in the executive power over foreign affairs through the advice and consent that they give to all treaties. As Madison puts it in Paper 63, the Senate is to, "… possess that sensibility to the opinion of the world, which is perhaps not less necessary in order to merit, than it is to obtain, the world's respect and confidence."

It's not only, Madison stresses in Paper 63, that senators are expected to be individuals who arrive at the Senate with superior qualifications. In addition, their collective as well as individual sense of responsibility or answerability, in the long run, is to be much greater than that of members of the House, because the smallness of their number, the length of their term, and their resulting conspicuousness and their greater involvement in foreign policy will make them held more individually accountable by the people and by history.

At the same time Madison shows, in Paper 63, that he expects the Senate will be independent enough of the people to be able to check and balance not only the House, but even the American people as a whole, or their public opinion. The Senate is to be what Madison calls, in his words, "an anchor against popular fluctuations." Especially in what Madison calls those "particular moments in public affairs, when the people, stimulated by some irregular passion, or some illicit advantage, or misled by the artful misrepresentations of interested men, may call for measures which they themselves will afterwards be the most ready to lament and condemn."

In our next lecture, we will listen to the critical response the Anti-Federalists give to this Madisonian vision of the proposed constitution's dynamic separation of powers.

# Lecture Ten

# Disputing Separation of Powers, Part 2

**Scope:** The Anti-Federalist refusal to go along with this whole scheme expresses their insistence on greater reliance on the people and less reliance on leaders and institutional arrangements. Alarmed at the monarchic character of the proposed Presidency, the Anti-Federalists argue for an executive council instead. Hamilton defends the powerful unitary Presidency on the grounds of what is required for adequately energetic and unified domestic administration as well as leadership in foreign policy.

## Outline

I. The Anti-Federalists' reply to Madison's argument about the true meaning of "separation of powers" is that both he and the Federalists betray a fundamental misunderstanding of Montesquieu's teaching.

  A. Montesquieu expresses his theory as a systematic explanation of the British Constitution, as Madison and Hamilton indicate, but the Anti-Federalists protest that the British Constitution is monarchic, not republican.

     1. The British system of separation of powers and checks and balances depends on distributing departments of power into the distinct hands of permanently different and competing social classes.

     2. In this way the system has deeply rooted social guarantees against the different institutions coalescing.

  B. In America, however, there is no such social basis that can be relied upon to maintain the permanent separation and competition of the major institutions. In the proposed constitution, the distinctions between the executive and legislative branches are merely artificial, with no basis in social reality.

II. This expresses the Anti-Federalist position that checking and balancing should be between the state and central governments.

  A. This would both ensure a truer checking and balancing and would strengthen government that is more local.

**B.** Any danger posed by the House of Representatives would be most reliably checked by greater power being given to the states and less power to the federal government.

**C.** Underlying this is a deeper Anti-Federalist preference for relying less on complex government and more on a simpler government directly responsive to and easily comprehended by the people.

**D.** In general, the Anti-Federalists see the proposed constitutional system as falling between two stools.

    **1.** It fails to meet the standards of the Montesquieuan doctrine centered on admiration for the British Constitution.

    **2.** It fails to make sufficient use of the more truly republican forms of checking and balancing.

**E.** The Anti-Federalists see the attempt to create artificial substitutes for the competing, class-based institutions of England as likely to fail and to result in a more oligarchic federal government.

**F.** The Anti-Federalists are especially skeptical of the proposed Senate.

    **1.** Where Madison sees an assembly of elder statesman counteracting populism, the Anti-Federalists see "a monster [of] baneful aristocracy, which will swallow up the democratic rights and liberties of the nation."

    **2.** The Anti-Federalist worry is focused not only on the elitist character of the Senate but also on what they see as the frightening violation of the principle of separation of powers that gives the Senate so crucial a share in the judicial and executive branches.

    **3.** The Anti-Federalists warn that these powers make it likely that the Senate will coalesce with the Presidency either by dominating the President or creating a party within the Senate that will allow the President to make it his tool.

    **4.** Even some leading Federalists confess unease at the design of the Senate.

**III.** Anti-Federalist alarm about the powers of the proposed Senate makes the Anti-Federalist view of the Presidency more complicated and divided.

**A.** Most Anti-Federalists voice a pretty simple and straightforward fear of what they see as the excessive and ill-defined powers given to the office of the Presidency, which they see as posing the threat of monarchic despotism.

B.  Strong worry is voiced about the constitution's open-ended wording of the grant of the executive power to the President, which might mean that the President can interpret and apply the laws as he wishes.

C.  The Anti-Federalists recognize and concede that the nature of executive power demands greater unity, forcefulness, and secrecy than either legislative or judicial power.

   1.  What is proposed by most of the Anti-Federalists is a small executive council, the chairman of which would be the chief executive but whose members would be elected by the people.

   2.  In their argument for a plural executive, the Anti-Federalists appeal to examples of classical republican tradition, none of which ever had a single chief executive as powerful or unrestricted as the proposed President.

D.  Some Anti-Federalists express fear not that the President will be too strong but rather that he will be too weak to balance the potentially oligarchic legislature and judiciary.

E.  The Anti-Federalists, in their proposals for an executive council with a single powerful chairman, wrestle to conceive of an executive branch that will avoid the danger of monarchic power while strengthening the balancing power of a more trustworthy executive.

IV.  To all these worries about the proposed Presidential office, Hamilton begins the Federalist reply with a rejection of the deceitful idea that the proposed Presidency is tantamount to a monarchic office.

A.  In *Federalist* 69, Hamilton proves that there is a vast difference between the powers and role assigned the proposed Presidency and the much greater powers of the limited English monarch.

B.  In *Federalist* 70, however, Hamilton acknowledges that in the classical republics, single chief executives have generally been avoided.

C.  Hamilton's defense is mainly on the grounds of what effective governing requires.

   1.  Those who attack the proposed Presidency on account of its strength imply that republican liberty cannot be made safely

compatible with a "vigorous executive," which would mean that republican liberty is incompatible with good government.

2. Energy requires a single chief who wields full command and final responsibility; in contrast, an executive council will inevitably lead to divisions at the highest level.

3. The dispersion of authority in a plural executive council does not strengthen responsibility but instead weakens it.

4. It is therefore actually a single chief executive who is more easily made subject to the people's ultimate judgment and control.

**D.** Also required for the sake of energy and responsibility in the executive is a considerable duration of the term of office in order to give the executive the necessary amount of independence.

1. In *Federalist* 72, Hamilton argues for the benefits of making the President eligible for reelection, arguing for the need to make the officeholder's concern for the long-term public good reinforced by the prospect of long-term personal spiritual rewards for himself.

2. Hamilton highlights the Federalist insistence on the healthiness of the ambition expected to animate those individuals who seek the highest national office.

3. Responding to Anti-Federalist worries about a coalescence of the Senate and the President in an oppressive, aristocratic elite, Hamilton reiterates the Federalist insistence that "the institution of delegated power implies that there is a portion of virtue and honour among mankind, which may be a reasonable foundation of confidence ..."

## Essential Reading:

"The Federal Farmer," 13<sup>th</sup>–15<sup>th</sup> Letters; in Storing, *The Complete Anti-Federalist*, Vol. 2, pp. 301–23.

*The Federalist*, Papers 67–77.

## Supplementary Reading:

Thatch, *The Creation of the Presidency*, Chapters 4–5.

**Questions to Consider:**

1. Which of the two competing sides seems to you to give a more convincing interpretation of the meaning of Montesquieu's doctrine of separation and division of powers?

2. After considering Hamilton's defense of the Presidency, how much truth, if any, do you find in the Anti-Federalist accusation that the office is essentially monarchic?

# Lecture Ten—Transcript
## Disputing Separation of Powers, Part 2

In the last lecture we followed Madison's argument about the true meaning of the "separation of powers" as taught by Montesquieu, his criticism of the Anti-Federalists for misunderstanding Montesquieu's teaching, and Madison's defense of the proposed constitution's way of embodying the checks and balances that are the key purpose of the separation of powers.

The Anti-Federalists' reply by insisting that it is Madison and the Federalists who betray a fundamental misunderstanding, or else a willful misapplication, of Montesquieu's great teaching—for Montesquieu expresses his theory as a systematic explanation of the British Constitution, as Madison and Hamilton repeatedly indicate themselves. To quote Madison, in Paper 47:

> The British Constitution was to Montesquieu ... the perfect model from which the principles and rules ... were to be drawn, and by which all similar works were to be judged. This great political critic appears to have viewed the Constitution of England as the standard, or to use his own expression, as the mirror of political liberty; and to have delivered, in the form of elementary truths, the several characteristic principles of that particular system.

But, the Anti-Federalists then protest, the British Constitution is monarchic, not republican, and the whole system of British separation of powers, checks and balances, absolutely depends on distributing departments of power into the distinct hands of permanently different and competing social classes or orders: the executive in the hands of a hereditary monarch and his family, and the legislative power divided between a hereditary nobility in the House of Lords, and the common people in the House of Commons, with the supreme judiciary power in the hands of a portion of the hereditary House of Lords.

In this way, the Anti-Federalists point out, a system like that has real, deeply rooted social guarantees against the different institutions coalescing. It is certain in such a system that the various institutions will not coalesce, because each institution is in the hands of a distinct class or social order, orders whose permanent interests conflict with one another.

But in America there is no such social basis that can be relied on to maintain the permanent separation and competition of the major institutions. There is no sufficient guarantee in the class interests of the members of the different branches, that they will not amalgamate in some kind of an oligarchic elite against the interests of the people. In this proposed constitution, the distinctions between the holders of the executive and legislative branches, and even more between the members of the two chambers of the legislative branch, are merely artificial, nothing but ideal constructs on paper, with no basis in social reality. As Patrick Henry says, in one of his great orations against the constitution:

> Tell me not of checks on paper; but tell me of checks founded on self-love. The English government is founded on self-love ... It has interposed that hereditary nobility between the king and the commons ... Compare this with your congressional checks ... Where are your checks? You have no hereditary nobility ... because, as Montesquieu says, when you give titles of nobility, you know what you give; but when you give power, you know not what you give ... In the British government there are real balances and checks: in this system there are only ideal balances.

Or as "The Federal Farmer" puts it, in his 11th letter in this proposed constitution, he says:

> The members of both houses must generally be the same kind of men ... the partitions between the two branches will be merely those of the building in which they sit. There will not be found in them any of those genuine balances and checks, among the real different interests ... nor can any such balances and checks be formed in the present condition of the United States in any considerable degree of perfection.

"The Federal Farmer" goes on to propose a fundamental redesign of the Senate, to make the senators more truly the delegates of their respective state governments; above all, by making the senators dismissible by their state governments.

This, of course, expresses the Anti-Federalist position that checking and balancing should be not only, or even mainly, within the central government—to try to imitate Montesquieu's system is a hopeless task in America—rather, between the state and the central governments. There you have a real basis. That would both ensure a truer checking and balancing, and would strengthen government that is more local and closer to the people.

Any danger posed by the House of Representatives, such as Madison worries about, would be most reliably checked not by creating another artificially aristocratic legislative chamber such as the proposed Senate, but rather by greater power being given to the states and less power to the federal government and thus to the House.

Since the Anti-Federalists regard even the House of Representatives as already too aristocratic in itself, they are left cold by the Federalist argument that a still more aristocratic Senate is needed to check the House's populist proclivities. As we've seen, in the Anti-Federalist view, the House ought to be made more populist by having annual elections, for a larger number of members, and the House should be given more power to allow it to predominate.

Underlying this is a deeper Anti-Federalist preference for relying less on complex government, of internal checks and balances, and relying instead more on simpler government directly responsive to and derived from and understandable by the people, easily comprehended by the people. This outlook is best expressed in the first letter of "Centinel," where he writes:

> The form of government which holds those entrusted with power in the greatest responsibility to their constituents is the best. ... The highest responsibility is to be attained in a simple structure of government; for the great body of the people never steadily attend to the operations of government, and for want of due information are liable to be imposed on. If you complicate the plan by various orders, the people will be perplexed and divided in their sentiments about the source of abuses or misconduct: some will impute it to the Senate, others to the House, and so on; and the interposition of the people may be rendered imperfect or perhaps wholly abortive. But if, imitating the Constitution of Pennsylvania, you vest all the legislative power in one body of men separating the executive and judicial, elected for a short period, and necessarily excluded by rotation from permanency ... you will create the most perfect responsibility: for then, whenever the people feel a grievance, they cannot mistake the authors, and will apply the remedy with certainty and effect, discarding them at the next election.

In general, the Anti-Federalists see the proposed constitutional system as falling between two stools. On the one hand, it fails to meet the standards of the Montesquieuan doctrine, centered on admiration for the monarchic British Constitution, which has far better guarantees of permanent separation and competition among the powers of government, by distributing the powers internally among distinct and antagonistic social orders. On the other hand, the proposed constitution fails to make sufficient use of the more truly republican forms of checking and balancing, namely federalism, which requires creating an equilibrium between state and federal government and which facilitates keeping government directly responsible to and reflective of the people, which means relying less on internal checks and balances and more on making government simple, with power weighted toward the popularly elected and controlled legislatures.

The Anti-Federalists see the attempt, in the proposed constitution, to create artificial substitutes for the competing class-based institutions of England as likely to fail and to result in simply a more oligarchic, consolidated federal government.

The Anti-Federalists are especially skeptical of the proposed Senate, which Madison sees, in this proposed Senate, as an assembly of elder statesmen, counteracting populism. The Anti-Federalists decry the Senate as, in the words of a New York writer who signs himself "Cincinnatus," "a monster" of "baneful aristocracy, which will swallow up the democratic rights and liberties of the nation."

The Anti-Federalist worry is focused not only on the elitist character of the Senate in itself, but on what they see as this frightening violation of the principle of separation of powers, that gives the Senate so crucial a share in the judicial, and still worse, in the executive, branches through this assigned role of giving advice and consent to treaties and thus becoming deeply involved in foreign policy, and through the assigned role of giving advice and consent to all the President's senior appointments in the executive branch.

As this writer "Cincinnatus" says, "… we have seen powers, in every branch of government, in violation of all principle, and all safety, condensed in this aristocratic Senate." Repeatedly the Anti-Federalists warn these powers that intrude the Senate into the executive sphere make it all too likely that the Senate will coalesce with the President, either by dominating the President, making him a tool of the oligarchic Senate, or else by forcing the President to use the perquisites of his office to seduce and corrupt enough Senators to create a party of his own within the Senate that will allow the President to make it his tool. To substantiate this worry with historical evidence, the Anti-Federalists point to the way the British king, under the "system of bribery introduced by his prime minister, Sir

Robert Walpole," had thus corrupted the British Parliament in the early 18$^{th}$ century.

Either way, Anti-Federalists fear, an oligarchic combination will form that will overwhelm the House. Thus "Centinel" warns in his first letter, "The President, who would be a mere pageant of state, unless he coincides with the views of the Senate, would either become the head of the aristocratic junto in that body, or its minion."

Even some leading Federalists confessed unease at the design of the Senate. Thus James Wilson, who had played a leading constructive role in the constitutional convention, and who was the principal defender in Pennsylvania of the proposed constitution, said in a major speech in the Pennsylvania ratifying convention, "I confess, I wish the powers of the Senate were not as they are. I think it would have been better if those powers had been distributed in other parts of the system."

Madison himself, months later, in a speech he made in the first Congress, conceded looking back retrospectively that, in his words, "Perhaps there was no argument urged with more success, or more plausibly grounded against the Constitution, under which we are now deliberating, than that found in the mingling of the executive and legislative branches of the government in one body." That is, in his favorite, the Senate.

This Anti-Federalist alarm about the powers of the proposed Senate, and their fear more generally of oligarchic tendencies in any national legislature, even in the House of Representatives, makes the Anti-Federalist view of the Presidency more complicated and divided. Of course, it is no surprise to see that most of the Anti-Federalists voice a pretty simple and straightforward fear of what they see as the excessive and ill-defined powers given to this office of the Presidency, which they see as posing a threat of monarchic despotism. They follow a deep worry that was expressed by Benjamin Franklin, in a major speech that he delivered in writing early in the convention itself. There he put his warning in these words, "There is a natural inclination in mankind to kingly government. It sometimes relieves them from aristocratic domination. ... I am apprehensive therefore, perhaps too apprehensive, that the government of these States may, in future times, end in monarchy."

A few days later, in the convention, George Mason had spoken in horror of the proposal for a single chief executive with his veto power over the legislation:

We are not indeed [he said] constituting a British government, but a more dangerous monarchy, an elective one. We are introducing a new principle into our system. ... I never could agree to give up all the rights of the people to a single magistrate. If more than one had been fixed on, then greater powers might be entrusted to the executive.

In particular, strong worry is voiced about the constitution's open-ended wording of the grant of the executive power to the President. Will this not mean in practice, some Anti-Federalists ask, that the President can interpret and apply the laws as he wishes? Thus William Symmes of Massachusetts asks, "Is there no instance in which he may reject the sense of the legislature, and establish his own? And so far, would he not be to all intents and purposes absolute?"

The Anti-Federalists do recognize and concede that the nature of the executive power, especially in domestic emergencies and wartime, demands much greater unity and decisive forcefulness and secrecy than does either the legislative or judicial power. But what is proposed by most of the Anti-Federalists, led by George Mason and "Centinel," as well as "The Federal Farmer," is a small executive council. The chairman of which would be the chief executive as first among equals, but whose others members would be elected by the people, independently of the President, to advise and share executive power and responsibility. Thus avoiding a monarchic executive, by making the President only the chairman of an executive committee and thus also avoiding what the dissenting minority at the Pennsylvania Convention calls the "dangerous and improper mixture of the executive with the legislative" that's involved in the role of the proposed Senate. Because if there was an executive counsel, the Senate wouldn't have to give its advice and consent to treaties, the council could; and similarly to appointments.

In their argument for a plural executive, here again the Anti-Federalists appeal to the entire historical record, all the great historical examples of the classical republican tradition, none of which ever had a single chief executive anywhere near as powerful as this proposed President. The Roman Republic, which flourished for centuries, fighting, of course, many successful wars, always had a dual consulship and a plural tribunate. When that was eventually abolished in favor of a single council by Augustus Caesar, it signaled the death knell of the republic and the beginning of the empire.

Athens always had an executive council, the Prytaneum. Sparta had four chief executives, two kings for the conduct of war, two ephors for domestic administration. In medieval and modern times, the great republics of Italy and northern Europe have never allowed such power in the hands of a single chief executive. The Venetian doge, for example, was notoriously weak.

The complexity of the Anti-Federalist's position appears when we find that some of the Anti-Federalists, a significant minority, expressed the contrary fear; not that the President will be too strong, but rather that he'll be too weak, or insufficiently independent, to balance the potentially oligarchic legislature and judiciary. Thus John Mercer of Maryland writes, "the only remedy the ingenuity of man has discovered for this evil [of oligarchy] is— a properly constituted and independent executive, an avenger of public wrongs." Mercer was driven so far as to argue for a chief executive elected for life, "whose person," Mercer writes, "must be sacred from impeachment," and who would appoint the members of the Senate.

Richard Henry Lee expresses the hope that the chief executive, while he should be chair of an executive council independent of the Senate, would tower above his colleagues and be a powerfully popular leader, to whom the people might rally; perhaps because he would be more directly elected than in the proposed electoral college system. Such a national leader, Lee suggests, would not only pose a counterweight to the dangerous oligarchic tendencies of the legislature, especially in the Senate, but would also, Henry Lee points out, prevent or counter the tendency to fragmentation of public opinion around competing powerful regional or state leaders, military heroes or others, powerful individuals in the various states, who, in the absence of a single, popular executive leader in the national government, might become successful revolutionary regional demagogues.

"The Federal Farmer" most eloquently expresses this rather fascinating minority Anti-Federalist view in his 14th letter, where he writes that history shows that:

> The people usually point out a first man … who must be a visible point serving as a common centre in the government, towards which to draw their eyes and attachments … superior in the opinion of the people to the most popular men in the different parts of the community, else the people will be apt to divide and follow their respective leaders. Aspiring men, armies and navies, have not often been kept in tolerable order by the decrees of a senate or an executive council. … A council will generally consist of the

aristocracy, and not stand so indifferent between it and the people as will a first magistrate.

"The Federal Farmer" goes on to admit that his colleagues, his fellow Anti-Federalists, worry about the monarchic implications of such a preeminent individual. But he responds, "Our executive may be altogether elective, and possess no power, but as the substitute of the people, and that well limited, and only for a limited time." So, "The Federal Farmer" concludes by calling for a short Presidential term of office, and frequent elections.

We thus find the Anti-Federalists in their proposals for an executive council with a single powerful chairman wrestling to conceive simultaneously an executive branch that will avoid the danger of excessively monarchic power, while strengthening the balancing power of a more trustworthy and more popular or democratic executive.

To all these worries about the proposed Presidential office, Alexander Hamilton begins the Federalist reply, in Paper 67, with an unusually impassioned, indignant rejection of what he characterizes as the totally unfair and deceitful charge that the proposed Presidency is tantamount to a monarchic office. In Paper 69, Hamilton easily proves that there is a vast difference between the powers and role assigned the proposed President and the much greater powers of even the limited English monarch.

But, in Paper 70, Hamilton has to acknowledge that, in the history of republicanism, and especially classical republics, single, independent chief executives with terms of more than a few months have generally been avoided. An Anti-Federalist might well wonder whether the opening passion of Hamilton's defense does not betray a certain defensiveness or sense of vulnerability on this point. Is Hamilton not, after all, an Anti-Federalist might well ask, seeking to incorporate into the new American republicanism at least important ingredients of the monarchic tradition?

Certainly Hamilton's defense of this Presidency is not mainly on grounds of it being republican or what republicanism requires, but rather on the grounds of what effective governing requires. He makes that very clear at the end of Paper 77. He argues in Paper 70 that those who attack the proposed Presidency on account of its strength are making an argument that endangers the very cause of republicanism, because the implication is, Hamilton claims, that republican liberty cannot be made safely compatible with what Hamilton calls, a "vigorous executive." If that were true, Hamilton says, that would mean that republican liberty is incompatible with good government. For as Hamilton explains in the famous words of Paper 70:

> Energy in the executive is a leading character in the definition of good government. It is essential to the protection of the community against foreign attacks: it is not less essential to the steady administration of the laws; to the protection of property against those irregular and high-handed combinations which sometimes interrupt the ordinary course of justice; to the security of liberty against the enterprises and assaults of ambition, of faction, and of anarchy.

Energy requires, Hamilton goes on to argue, a single chief, who wields full command and final responsibility. In contrast, an executive council will inevitably lead to divisions at the highest level, which, as Hamilton puts it, "lessen the respectability, weaken the authority, and distract the plans and operations of those whom they divide."

In addition, Hamilton points out, the dispersion of authority in a plural executive council does not strengthen responsibility to the people, but instead weakens or undermines such responsibility because it makes it difficult or impossible for the people, or public opinion, to judge who is responsible for controversial executive decisions or conduct. The members of a council would each have a strong incentive to disavow their own responsibility for unpopular or unsuccessful measures, and foist the blame on the other members.

It's therefore actually, Hamilton argues, a single chief executive who is more easily made subject to the people's ultimate judgment and control. In Paper 71, Hamilton shows that he expects, under the system proposed, that the electoral college will make the Presidential elections an expression of the people's judgment on the sitting President. But that means, implies, also required for the sake of energy and responsibility in the executive, as Hamilton contends in Paper 71, is a considerable duration of the term of office, in order to give the executive the necessary amount of independence so that the President will be willing to take temporarily unpopular stands. So that he will be able to maintain his independence in the struggle of checks and balances with the legislature, for which his qualified veto power is his main weapon and shield, as Hamilton points out in Paper 73. The veto power is also, as Hamilton puts it, something that "furnishes an additional security against the enaction of improper laws."

In Paper 72, Hamilton argues further for the benefits of making the President eligible for reelection, arguing not only on all the previous grounds that I've just gone through and not only on grounds that reelection will bring in stability and experience but, in addition, because of the need to make the office holder's concern for the long-term public good reinforced by the prospect of long-term personal spiritual rewards for himself. Above all, the spiritual reward that satisfies what Hamilton calls, "the love of fame, the ruling passion of the noblest minds, which would prompt a man to plan, and undertake, extensive and arduous enterprises for the public benefit, requiring considerable time to mature and perfect them."

Hamilton thus highlights the Federalist insistence on the healthiness of the ambition, the love of fame that is expected to animate those individuals who seek the highest national office. Similarly, in responding to the Anti-Federalist worries about a coalescence of the Senate and the President in an oppressive oligarchic aristocratic junto or elite, Hamilton reiterates the Federalist insistence that, as he puts it:

> The institution of delegated power implies that there is a portion of virtue and honour among mankind, which may be a reasonable foundation of confidence. ... A man disposed [he says] to view human nature as it is, without either flattering its virtues, or exaggerating its vices, will see sufficient ground of confidence in the probity of the Senate, to rest satisfied, not only that it will be impracticable to the executive to corrupt or seduce a majority of its members, but that the necessity of its cooperation, in the business of appointments, will be a considerable and salutary restraint upon the conduct of that chief executive magistrate.

This moderate degree of Federalist trust in the virtue of which at least some rare individuals are capable, is nowhere more evident than in Hamilton's defense of the proposed constitution's judiciary and Supreme Court in Papers 78 and following. Here again we find that where the Federalists see good grounds to bestow the country's trust, the Anti-Federalists see an imprudent and dangerous opening to aristocratic subversion of the democratic republic.

In our next lecture, we will follow Hamilton's great articulation of the defensive argument for judicial review, and for the other powers of the proposed federal judiciary. We'll consider the strengths and weaknesses of Hamilton's argument as these become evident in the light of the Anti-Federalist attack on the proposed judiciary.

# Lecture Eleven
# The Supreme Court and Judicial Review

**Scope:** Hamilton's expectation of superior virtues in the national leadership becomes more evident in his defense of the unelected, life-tenured Supreme Court and its historically unprecedented power of judicial review: the ability to declare laws void because they are unconstitutional. The Anti-Federalists predict that this power will be abused by the Supreme Court to dominate the system. They insist that the proper highest authority on the meaning of the constitution in a democracy should be a body that includes elected officials.

# Outline

I. Hamilton's stress on the need for a prudent degree of trust becomes especially evident in his defense of the proposed constitution's judiciary and Supreme Court from Paper 78 onward. Where the Federalists see reasonable grounds to place the country's trust in selected individuals of superior moral and intellectual qualities, the Anti-Federalists see a dangerous opening to aristocratic subversion of the democratic republic.

II. The Anti-Federalists have several different worries about the proposed national judiciary.

   A. They see the federal judiciary as designed to help weaken popular jury authority, not least by the explicit granting to the higher courts power to review and overturn jury judgments of fact as well as law.

   B. They see the jurisdiction of the federal courts as going far beyond what is necessary in a federal system and fear that the federal courts will dominate and render impotent state courts.

   C. The most fundamental complaint is about the extremely undemocratic power of the Supreme Court because it is an unelected body making decisions over which neither the people nor the people's representatives have any say and because of judicial review: the judiciary's power to declare null and void laws that have been duly enacted by the people's representatives.

1. "Brutus" is the first to articulate the full meaning of judicial review in the American system.
2. "Brutus" contends that to be given the power to judge constitutional cases according to "equity" means to be given the power to judge according to the spirit of the law and in accordance with the implicit intention of the original lawgiver.
3. "Brutus" argues that it follows that this power is given to the judicial courts and no other branch.
4. If the people adopt this constitution, he warns, they should realize that they will be subordinating their own elected representatives to the judiciary.

III. In response to "Brutus," Hamilton defends the proposed judiciary and, in Paper 78, builds his own case for the reasonableness of the power of judicial review.

A. Hamilton asserts that the judicial branch "will always be the least dangerous to the political rights of the constitution; because it will be least in a capacity to annoy or injure them."
1. Hamilton's claim as to the minimal danger of the judiciary is hotly disputed by leading Anti-Federalists.
2. Hamilton appeals to the authority of Montesquieu, who spoke of the judiciary as so comparatively weak as to be "next to nothing" in power compared to the legislative and executive branches; yet in Montesquieu's discussion, there is no hint of a power in the judiciary to declare laws unconstitutional.

B. Though Hamilton introduces and recognizes that the proposed judiciary is intended to have the power of judicial review, he denies what he calls "the imagination, that the doctrine would imply a superiority of the judiciary to the legislative power."
1. It is not perfectly clear that Hamilton ever successfully refutes this conclusion.
2. At the heart of his own explanation, Hamilton says that the judiciary has been "designed ... in order, among other things, to keep the [legislators] within the limits assigned to their authority."

C. Hamilton claims to prove that judicial review is an expression of the supreme power of the majority will of the people.
1. Representative government has no legitimate authority to exceed its lawful commission given by the people; in the

proposed American system, the people's commission will be the written constitution.

2. Any governmental action that violates the constitution will be a violation of the people's most fundamental will, constituting the political order; thus, to declare laws of the government null and void because contrary to the constitution is not opposing but enforcing the people's most basic intention and will.

3. This argument does not yet prove that it is the unelected Supreme Court that has been delegated by the people to have their final say in interpreting what the people intend their constitution to mean.

D. Hamilton's argument is that judicial review is intrinsic to a constitution that expresses the will of the people where that popular will is more authoritative than even the will of the people's elected representative government.

E. Why is it the courts that have the supreme and final say in interpreting what the people mean by their constitution?

1. Hamilton points to the Anti-Federalist argument, which says that the part of government best suited to understand what the people mean and intend is the legislature; in contrast, unelected judges are not responsible to the people and not as qualified to know what is the people's understanding.

2. Hamilton counters this by saying that "it is far more rational to suppose, that the courts were designed to be an intermediate body between the people and the legislature, in order, among other things, to keep the latter within the limits assigned to their authority."

3. Hamilton appeals to what he claims is the nature of the judicial function, which is uniquely suited to interpreting laws, and therefore the constitution, as fundamental law.

IV. At the core of Hamilton's justification for judicial review is a new claim about the nature of the judiciary: The power of judicial review is intrinsic to the function of the judiciary.

A. This implies that the judges are uniquely qualified to exercise such power, but as the Anti-Federalists stress, this seems an aristocratic argument, not a democratic one.

B. The aristocratic character of Hamilton's argument becomes more plausible when he notes, in Paper 78, that the Supreme Court will sometimes have to stand in opposition not only to the legislature but also to the will of the people at times when the public is temporarily corrupted into threatening the rights of minorities or individuals against the underlying principles of the constitution.

C.  Hamilton makes clear that the Federalists are relying on superior virtues in the judges—both intellectual virtues that will endow them with a superior capacity of insight and moral virtues that will enable them to assert and defend the most fundamental intention of the people, even against what the people think their most fundamental intention is.

D.  Hamilton thus conceives of the federal judiciary as a kind of needed aristocracy whose special virtues are in service to the people and their fundamental will.

E.  The full scope of Hamilton's conception of this aristocratic role emerges only when we see he is quietly indicating that the intention is for the courts to protect not only the constitution but rights not necessarily in the constitution and general unwritten principles of justice.

**Essential Reading:**

"Brutus," 11$^{th}$, 14$^{th}$, and 15$^{th}$ Essays; in Storing, *The Complete Anti-Federalist*, Vol. 2, pp. 433–42.

"The Federal Farmer," 13$^{th}$–15$^{th}$ Letters; in Storing, *The Complete Anti-Federalist*, Vol. 2, pp. 301–23.

*The Federalist*, Papers 78–81 (review Papers 44 and 48).

**Supplementary Reading:**

Slonim, "Federalist No. 78 and Brutus' Neglected Thesis on Judicial Supremacy."

**Questions to Consider:**

1.  To what extent does today's functioning of the Supreme Court bear out the predictions of each side in the debate over its likely character?

2.  What are the strengths and the weaknesses of the arguments of "Brutus" and Hamilton over the legitimacy of judicial review?

# Lecture Eleven—Transcript
## The Supreme Court and Judicial Review

At the end of the last lecture, I suggested that Hamilton's stress on the need for a prudent degree of trust in the virtue of which some rare individuals are capable becomes especially evident in his defense of the proposed constitution's judiciary and Supreme Court in Papers 78 and following. Here again we find that where the Federalists see reasonable grounds to place the country's trust in selected individuals of superior moral and intellectual qualities, the distrustful Anti-Federalists see an imprudent and dangerous opening to aristocratic subversion. "The Federal Farmer" goes so far as to declare that, as he puts it in his 15ᵗʰ letter, "... we may fairly conclude, we are more in danger of sowing the seeds of arbitrary government in this department," referring to the proposed judiciary, "than in any other."

The Anti-Federalists have several different worries about the proposed national judiciary, culminating in the Supreme Court. For one thing, they see the federal judiciary, as we've seen in earlier lectures, designed to help weaken popular jury authority, not least by the explicit grant of the higher courts' power to review and overturn jury judgments of fact, as well as law.

For another thing, they see the jurisdiction of the federal courts as going far beyond what is necessary in a federal system and they fear that as a result, the federal courts will totally dominate and render impotent the state courts.

But the most fundamental, far-reaching, and far-sighted complaint is about the extremely undemocratic or aristocratic power of the Supreme Court. Both because it is an unelected body with lifetime appointments, exercising final appeal, deliberating in secret, and making decisions over which neither the people nor the people's elected representatives have any say; and still worse, on account of what we nowadays call judicial review, or the judiciary's power—and at the summit, the Supreme Court's power—to declare null and void, "unconstitutional," laws that have been duly enacted by the people's elected representatives.

It is the Anti-Federalist "Brutus" who is the first to articulate the full meaning of what we call nowadays judicial review in the American system, and he does so in terms of great alarm. "Brutus" discovers judicial review on the basis of his analysis of the meaning of the following words of Article 3, Section 2 of the proposed constitution, defining the judicial power. The Constitution reads as follows: "the judicial power shall extend to all cases in law and equity arising under this constitution." "Brutus" contends that to be given the power to judge constitutional cases according to "equity" means—as is taught, he says, by great traditional authorities like Blackstone and Grotius—it means to be given the power to judge according to the spirit of the law, even outside or against the letter of the law. It also means to be given the power to judge in accordance with the implicit intention of the original lawgiver.

"Brutus" argues, it follows, from the fact that this power of judging according to equity as well as law is given explicitly to the federal courts and to no other part of the government, that this task is assigned to them, to the judicial branch and to no other branch. For no other branch or institution is given explicitly this power, by the wording of the proposed constitution; and in particular, the legislature is nowhere given such a power. Only the judiciary has the power to judge according to equity, the laws and the Constitution. Equity means the spirit and intention of the original founders. "Brutus" insists that, if the people adopt this constitution, he warns, they should realize that will be subordinating their own elected representatives to the judiciary, since it is the judiciary alone that is authorized explicitly to be the final interpreter of the meaning, the spirit, the intention of the constitution. In "Brutus's" words:

> In the exercise of this power they [meaning the federal judges] will not be subordinate to, but above the legislature. ... The legislature can only exercise such powers as are given them by the constitution, they can not assume any of the rights annexed to the judicial, for this plain reason, that the same authority which vested the legislature with their powers, vested the judicial with theirs. ... The supreme court then have a right, independent of the legislature, to give a construction to the constitution and every part of it, and there is no power provided in this system to correct their construction or do it away. If, therefore, the legislature pass any laws, inconsistent with the sense the judges put upon the constitution, they will declare it void; and therefore in this respect their power is superior to that of the legislature.

Then "Brutus" draws out in lurid terms what he regards as the frightening implications of this:

> I question [he writes] whether the world ever saw, in any period of it, a court of justice invested with such immense powers, and yet placed in a situation so little responsible. ... The judges in England

are under the control of the legislature, for they are bound to determine according to the laws passed by them. But the judges under this constitution will control the legislature, for the supreme court are authorized in the last resort, to determine what is the extent of the powers of the Congress; they are to give the constitution an explanation, and there is no power above them to set aside their judgment. ... They are independent of the people, of the legislature, and of every power under heaven. Men placed in this situation will generally soon feel themselves independent of heaven itself.

It's in response to this sounding of an alarm by "Brutus," an alarm which Hamilton actually quotes, in paraphrase, in *Federalist* Paper 81, that Hamilton is impelled to defend the proposed judiciary, and, in Paper 78, builds his own famous and very different case for the reasonableness of the power of judicial review. It is, of course, Hamilton's case for judicial review, built on later by John Marshall, rather than "Brutus's" which has become the canonical argument. But, Hamilton is only driven or provoked to make this case for judicial review because of the challenge posed by "Brutus."

Here, perhaps more than anywhere else, we see how importantly the Anti-Federalists contributed to the defining and articulation of the meaning of the Constitution precisely by their heated opposition to it and the provocation that caused.

Hamilton begins his defense of the proposed judicial power in Paper 78 by asserting, in phrases that have become famous, that the judicial branch, in his words, "will always be the least dangerous to the political rights of the constitution; because it will be least in a capacity to annoy or injure them." He goes on to explain the reason: The judiciary:

... has no influence over either the sword or the purse; no direction either of the strength or of the wealth of the society; and can take no active resolution whatever ... from [its] natural feebleness, it is in continual jeopardy of being overpowered, awed, or influenced by its coordinate branches.

This claim of Hamilton's, as to the minimal danger from the judiciary, is hotly disputed by the leading Anti-Federalists. Richard Henry Lee, writing as "The Federal Farmer," warns,

> The judges and juries, in their interpretations, and in directing the execution of them, have a very extensive influence for preserving

or destroying liberty, and for changing the nature of the government. ... Judicial power is of such a nature, that when we have ascertained and fixed its limits, with all the caution and precision we can, it will yet be formidable, somewhat arbitrary and despotic—that is, after all our cares, we must leave a vast deal to the discretion and interpretation—to the wisdom, integrity, and politics of the judges. ... When the legislature makes a bad law, or the first executive magistrate usurps upon the rights of the people, the people discover the evil much sooner, than the abuses of power in the judicial department; the proceedings of which are more intricate, complex, and out of the people's immediate view. A bad law immediately excites a general alarm; a bad judicial determination, though not less pernicious in its consequences, is immediately felt, probably, by a single individual only, and noticed only by his neighbors and a few spectators in the court.

One can wonder whether Hamilton ever really faces up to this argument warning against the potential power and, therefore, evils of the judiciary. There's even some reason to wonder if Hamilton is being altogether candid when he makes this initial and conspicuous claim of his, as to the relative weakness and hence innocuousness of the judiciary. Because Hamilton makes this claim about it being the least dangerous branch before he has admitted that "Brutus" is essentially correct in discerning that the proposed federal judiciary is designed to have the final, unappealable power to declare any law unconstitutional and thus void.

Something else indicates that Hamilton is not being entirely honest in this passage proclaiming the weakness of the judiciary under this constitution, because in a footnote to this passage, Hamilton appeals to and quotes the authority of Montesquieu. Now in his discussion of the judiciary, Montesquieu did indeed, as Hamilton quotes him here, speak of it as being so comparatively weak as to be "next to nothing" in power compared to the legislative and executive branches. Fair enough. But in Montesquieu's discussion, there is nowhere any hint of a power in the judiciary to declare laws unconstitutional.

In other words, Montesquieu is thinking of a judiciary as it appears in the British Constitution, where it has no such power. Hamilton misleadingly cites Montesquieu, as if Montesquieu were talking about a judiciary like the American, which has judicial review. Still, when Hamilton does go on to introduce and admit and recognize that the proposed judiciary is intended to have the power of judicial review, Hamilton repeatedly denies what he calls the "imagination, that the doctrine would imply a superiority of the judiciary to the legislative power."

"It is urged," Hamilton recognizes, referring, of course, to Brutus, "that the authority which can declare the acts of another void, must necessarily be superior to the one whose acts may be declared void." Hamilton denies that, but it's not perfectly clear that he ever successfully refutes this conclusion, which, as we've seen, is emphatically drawn by "Brutus."

At the heart of his own explanation of the judicial power, Hamilton says that the judiciary has been, in his words, "designed … in order, among other things, to keep the legislators within the limits assigned to their authority." Does this not sound like a superior's function? Does not an institution which is designed to keep another institution in its place sound like a superior, controlling the other as inferior? Can the doctrine of judicial review avoid the implication of judicial supremacy in some important degree, at least? Not, to be sure, in terms of physical power, power of the purse or sword, but in terms of legal and moral power? How is this enormous power of an unelected body, appointed for life, deliberating in secret, compatible with democratic republicanism? That's the question "Brutus" and the Anti-Federalists press.

How can one escape the Anti-Federalist conclusion that the Supreme Court is at least a somewhat aristocratic institution, designed to, at the least, check and limit the more democratic branches of government? Hamilton's response is to execute an amazing gambit. He claims to prove that judicial review is in fact, a democratic principle, an expression of the supreme power of the majority will of the people. How does he manage to make such an argument?

He begins from the premise that representative government has no legitimate authority to exceed its lawful commission given by the people. Then he adds that in the proposed American system, the people's commission will be the written constitution, adopted by the people, as their fundamental law, through the delegates they have elected in each state convention.

Therefore, any governmental action that violates the constitution will be a violation of the people's most fundamental will, constituting the political order and so, to declare laws or actions of the government null and void on the basis of their contravening the constitution is not opposing, but enforcing, the people's most basic intention and will.

The argument up to this point is very powerful, but unfortunately, it does not yet prove what Hamilton needs to prove because this argument does not yet prove that it is the unelected Supreme Court that has been delegated by the people to have the final say in interpreting what the people intend their constitution to mean. It is striking that Hamilton does not take advantage of the argument "Brutus" had made, to the effect that the wording of the proposed constitution's grant of judicial power, because of the use of the term "equity," itself implies that the courts are to have the final say in interpreting the constitution.

Hamilton apparently does not buy such an interpretation that so freighted a meaning was ever intended for the term "equity." In the subsequent Paper 81, Hamilton goes so far as to say that, in his words, "...there is not a syllable [in the Constitution] which directly empowers the national courts to construe the laws according to the spirit of the Constitution." He then adds that "this doctrine [of judicial review] is not deducible from any circumstance peculiar to the plan of the convention." So Hamilton wants to provide a justification that does not come from the text of the Constitution or from the convention. He wants to deduce judicial review from something more substantial and certainly more substantial than the mere meaning of this one word, "equity."

Hamilton's argument is that judicial review is intrinsic to the very idea of a constitution that expresses the will of the people, where that popular constitutional will is more authoritative than even the will of the people's elected representative government. But to repeat, the question then becomes, why is it the courts which have the supreme and final say in interpreting what the people mean by their constitution?

Here in Paper 78, Hamilton admits that one might suppose that, as he puts it, "the legislative body are themselves the constitutional judges of their own powers." In other words, Hamilton points to the Anti-Federalist argument which says the part of government best suited to understand what the people mean and intend by their constitution is the part that is elected by the people, the legislature. In contrast, judges, as unelected, as never having to stand for election or reelection, as never having to go out and campaign and get to know the people, are not responsible to the people and are not qualified as are the elected representatives, who have to campaign for election amongst the people, to know what is the people's understanding of their constitution's meaning. As "Brutus" says in his 15th and 16th essays:

> Had the construction of the Constitution been left with the legislature ... if they exceed their powers, or sought to find, in the spirit of the Constitution, more than was expressed in the letter, the people from whom they derived their power could remove them, and do themselves right; and indeed I can see no other remedy that the people can have against their rulers for encroachments of this nature. ... But when this power is lodged in the hands of men, independent of the people, and of their representatives, and who are not, constitutionally, accountable for their opinions, no way is left to control them. ... This supreme controlling power should be in the choice of the people, or else you establish an authority independent, and not amenable at all, which is repugnant to the principles of a free government. Agreeable to these principles, I suppose, the supreme judicial ought to be liable to be called to account, for any misconduct, by some body of men, who depend upon the people for their places.

Hamilton counters this by saying the following, "It is far more rational to suppose, that the courts were designed to be an intermediate body between the people and the legislature, in order, among other things, to keep the latter within the limits assigned to their authority." Why is it more rational to suppose this? The reason Hamilton proceeds to give is the following, in his famous key sentence:

> The interpretation of the laws is the proper and peculiar province of the courts. A constitution is in fact, and must be, regarded by the judges as a fundamental law. It therefore belongs to them to ascertain its meaning, as well as the meaning of any particular act proceeding from the legislative body.

In other words, Hamilton appeals to what he claims is implied in what he terms the "nature and reason of the thing," the nature of the judicial function, which is uniquely suited to interpreting laws and therefore the constitution as fundamental law. As he puts it later, in Paper 81:

> This doctrine is not deducible from any circumstance peculiar to the plan of the convention; but from the general theory of a limited constitution; and as far as it is true, is equally applicable to most, if not all, the state governments. There can be no objection, therefore, on this account, to the federal judicature, which will not lie against the local judicatures in general, and which will not serve to condemn every constitution that attempts to set bounds to legislative discretion.

Hamilton claims that the doctrine of judicial review applies to every republican constitutional order and in particular to all the states. But to this argument, "Brutus" has of course already protested that in none of the states, and certainly not in New York State, is there any such doctrine of judicial review as is being proposed in the new constitution according to Hamilton. "Brutus" in effect asks: If Hamilton is right about this doctrine being derived from the "general theory" of republican constitutionalism, then how come no republic has ever heard of this doctrine before in history, including the history of the 13 states?

At the core of Hamilton's justification for judicial review is a new claim about the nature of the judiciary, the claim that such power of judicial review is intrinsic to the function of the judiciary under a written constitution. This seems to mean that the judges are uniquely qualified to exercise such power. Judges alone are qualified to interpret the underlying spirit and meaning of the Constitution and the original or deepest intention of its framers, above all, the deepest intention of the people—both the people who originally ratified the Constitution through their delegates and the people in every subsequent generation who are continuing to accept it. This seems to mean that the basis of the whole doctrine is the special expertise and virtue of the judges.

But, as the Anti-Federalists have stressed, this seems an aristocratic argument, not a democratic argument. This aristocratic character of Hamilton's argument becomes still more plausible when Hamilton goes on to note, in Paper 78, that the Court will sometimes have to stand in opposition, not only to the will of the legislature or the agents of the people, but also to the manifest will of the people themselves, at times when the public or the majority is temporarily corrupted into threatening the rights of minorities or individuals, against the underlying principles of their constitution.

On such occasions, Hamilton writes, "it is easy to see, that it would require an uncommon portion of fortitude in the judges to do their duty as faithful guardians of the Constitution, where legislative invasions of it had been instigated by the major voice of the community." Hamilton thus makes clearer and clearer as he goes along that the Federalists are indeed relying on and hoping for superior virtues in the judges; both intellectual virtues of learning, in the law, jurisprudence, that will endow the judges with a superior capacity of insight into the full implications of what the people intended in their most solemn and fundamental civic act: the adopting and accepting of their constitution. Also moral virtues, virtues of heart or character, fortitude, as he says, that will enable the judges to assert and defend this most serious intention of the people, even against what may be a current mood or passion of the people. As Hamilton puts it:

> There can be but few men in the society who will have sufficient skill in the laws to qualify them for the stations of judges. And, making the proper deductions for the ordinary depravity of human nature, the number must be still smaller of those who unite the requisite integrity with the requisite knowledge.

Hamilton thus does conceive of the federal judiciary, especially in its exercise of the power of judicial review, as being a kind of needed aristocracy, but one whose special virtues are in service to the people, to the people's most fundamental and serious will.

In Paper 81, Hamilton replies to "Brutus's" argument that it would be wiser, better, more legitimate to vest the supreme interpretation of the Constitution in the legislature, as the people's elected representatives. His reply is based on challenging the qualifications, both intellectual and moral qualifications, for such a task, of elected representatives. "The members of the legislature," he writes, "will rarely be chosen with a view to those qualifications which fit men for the stations of judges," who are to be "men selected for their knowledge of the laws, acquired by long and laborious study." In addition, he points out that legislative bodies have, as he puts it, a "natural propensity [to] party divisions" and "the habit," he says, "of being continually marshaled on opposite sides, will be to apt to stifle the voice both of law and of equity," if legislatures are given the final constitutional say.

The full scope of Hamilton's conception of this aristocratic role of the federal courts emerges only when we see that he is quietly indicating that the intention is for the courts to protect not only the Constitution, but in addition, rights of individuals that are not necessarily in the Constitution, and in addition to that, general unwritten principles of justice. Thus Hamilton writes in Paper 78, that, in his words, "this independence of the judges is equally requisite to guard the Constitution and the rights of individuals." He makes it clear; it's not just the Constitution, it's something beyond that, the rights of individuals. Then he goes on to deliver the following most pregnant statement:

> But it is not with a view to infractions of the Constitution only, that the independence of the judges may be an essential safeguard against the effects of occasional ill humors in the society. These sometimes extend no farther than to the injury of the private rights

of particular classes of citizens, by unjust and partial laws. Here also the firmness of the judicial magistracy is of vast importance in mitigating the severity and confining the operation of such laws. It not only serves to moderate the immediate mischiefs of those which may have been passed, but it operates as a check upon the legislative body in passing them; who, perceiving that obstacles to the success of an iniquitous intention are to be expected from the scruples of the courts, are in a manner compelled, by the very motives of the injustice they meditate, to qualify their attempts. This is a circumstance calculated to have more influence upon the character of our governments, than but few may imagine.

In order to understand what Hamilton is hinting at here and getting at, we must bear in mind that he is assuming that there will be no Bill of Rights as part of the Constitution. He has in mind that the courts will, therefore, have to exercise a rather wide discretion, in applying unwritten and only implicit and traditional rules of equity and common law and perhaps even natural law and natural right.

This brings us to the last great bone of contention between Federalists and Anti-Federalists, namely, the Anti-Federalist complaint and expression of alarm at the fact that there is no formal, written, Bill or Declaration of Rights as part of the proposed Constitution. In our next and last lecture we will treat this great issue and see how it brings into focus some of the deepest ways in which each side has contributed to our American civic heritage.

# Lecture Twelve
## The Bill of Rights

**Scope:** The one great apparent victory of the Anti-Federalists is the addition, by the first Congress, of the amendments that constitute the Bill of Rights. Madison so redesigned the meaning and the contents of the Bill of Rights, however, that he got rid of much of what the Anti-Federalists hoped and intended for: provisions that would weaken the central government and restore greater independent power to the states. The argument over the Bill of Rights is a fitting conclusion to our study because it brings out characteristic strengths and weaknesses in the overall positions of the two sides.

## Outline

I. A leading feature of the Anti-Federalists' critique of the proposed constitution is their complaint about the absence of a Bill of Rights or their insistence that a Bill of Rights must be added in amendments to the proposed constitution.

    A. It was in this dimension of their critique that they tasted eventual victory and made their most famous contribution to our political tradition.

    B. This victory is not as substantial as it first seems.

        1. The Bill of Rights that was added by way of amendments drawn up in the first Congress under James Madison did not alter anything important in the proposed constitution.

        2. Madison's Bill of Rights strengthened the new Constitution and even gave to the central government important additional power contrary to the intention of the Anti-Federalists.

II. The agitation for a Bill of Rights began in the closing days of the Constitutional Convention.

    A. Starting with a proposal by Charles Pinckney of South Carolina, it had been decided to insert into relevant sections of the constitution statements of certain basic rights: the guarantee of the writ of habeas corpus, trial by jury in criminal cases, prohibitions on religious tests for office, ex post facto laws, and bills of attainder.

**B.** When the Convention was about to conclude, George Mason expressed his deep dismay that there was not a formal Bill of Rights; along with Elbridge Gerry, Mason moved that a Bill of Rights be drawn up.

**C.** The motion was unanimously voted down by all the delegations from the 10 states present.

    **1.** Some scholars have surmised that this was because the delegates feared that prolonged discussion would open up a large new field of difficulties and controversies.

    **2.** But the deeper reason was probably that this agitation for a Bill of Rights was seen by both sides as part of the broader effort by the Anti-Federalists to require amendments that would decisively weaken the proposed central government, and it was part of the Anti-Federalist campaign to weaken the people's trust in the proposed central government.

**III.** The Anti-Federalists have in mind something like what was found in the state bills of rights, the paradigm being the Virginia Declaration.

**A.** These bills, a legacy of the Revolutionary period, were radical documents.

    **1.** They included broad statements of political philosophy, elaborating the basic principles of justice and legitimate government based on the sovereignty of the people and stressing the people's right of revolutionary resistance to an oppressive government.

    **2.** These declarations were a legacy of the struggle against English domination and the earlier struggle within England against the oppressive prerogatives of the monarchy.

    **3.** These declarations breathe the spirit of distrust of government characteristic of the revolutionary movement.

**B.** The Anti-Federalists have in mind declarations that would include strong exhortations to civic virtue and religious piety, embodying the classical republican concern for popular virtue as a bulwark of freedom.

**C.** It is in this context that state declarations enumerate basic inalienable rights and freedoms that the central government is explicitly required to preserve as sacrosanct.

**D.** Jefferson and the Anti-Federalists want to include in the declaration specific and far-reaching prohibitions on what the central government can do.

    **1.** They want a prohibition on a professional army in peacetime and a statement affirming state militias as the backbone of the nation's defense.

    **2.** They want explicit limitations on the central government's powers to tax and regulate the economy.

    **3.** They want strong affirmations of states' rights.

**IV.** The Federalists quite rightly saw the agitation for a Bill of Rights as part of a larger movement aimed at weakening the constitution's forging of a powerful central government.

    **A.** The primary argument of the Federalists is that a Bill of Rights is not necessary.

        **1.** Historically, bills of rights have been needed to restrict the oppressive claims of monarchic government, but we no longer face such a government.

        **2.** It is not words of paper that really protect rights, it is the proper design of the constitution.

    **B.** A Bill of Rights would be, in crucial respects, risky.

        **1.** To lay down a list of rights that limit the government would carry the implication that the government would otherwise have legitimate power to infringe on basic rights, but the proposed constitution is based on the principle that all rights and powers not explicitly given to the government are kept by the people.

        **2.** If you compose an official listing of basic rights, it will be impossible to encompass all of them; whichever rights are not on the list may be regarded by future generations as not having a constitutional claim to protection.

    **C.** The Anti-Federalists have a powerful response.

        **1.** With Jefferson, they argue for the civic educational importance of an established statement of the most basic rights, which can include some cautionary statement that there are other rights not listed.

        **2.** This consideration played a major role in winning James Madison over to Jefferson's side.

**V.** What happened to bring about the amendments that constitute the Bill of Rights as we have them?

    **A.** Many Federalists, above all James Madison, became persuaded that if the statement of rights was properly crafted, then such a statement would do more good than harm.

        **1.** Madison recognized that in the wake of the Great Debate, there was widespread distrust about the Constitution among the minority who had supported the Anti-Federalist side.

        **2.** If there was added a Bill of Rights whose language was crafted in such a way that it did not weaken the new government, foster distrust, and stress the right of resistance, then it would go a long way in reassuring the opponents.

    **B.** The Bill of Rights as it emerged from Congress omitted most of what the Anti-Federalists had hoped would be included.

        **1.** Madison did use the amendments as a forum for expressing and teaching certain fundamental rights but omitted all language that would tie those rights to any specific political philosophy.

        **2.** By keeping the Bill of Rights detached from any specific philosophical or theological grounding, Madison facilitated popular reverence for and attachment to the Constitution for its own sake.

    **C.** Whereas the Anti-Federalists had tended to want a Bill of Rights that taught people to look at the federal government as a potential threat, Madison formulated a Bill of Rights that reassured people of their rights being respected and protected by the federal government.

**VI.** In the debate over the Bill of Rights are expressed some of the major strengths and weaknesses, and the most important legacy of each side.

    **A.** The Federalists deservedly won the Great Debate because they successfully defended a well-designed frame of governmental power, while the Anti-Federalists lost because they lacked a convincing alternative proposal.

    **B.** The Anti-Federalists, in their critique, help us to see what has had to be left out, and they alert us to some dangers that lurk in this new order as a result.

**C.** The Anti-Federalists were the first to voice in a serious way a set of worries that have played a healthy critical role in our civic tradition.

    **1.** They warn of a tendency in large-scale, centralized government to become oppressive.

    **2.** They plead for the spiritual value of strong local institutions that foster direct participation in self-government.

    **3.** Though they failed to appreciate how the Constitution was designed to achieve a central government that was both energetic and safe, they expressed what was to become widespread dissatisfaction at the insufficient amount of direct popular control over the national government.

**D.** The most important Anti-Federalist contribution is the highlighting of the insufficient attention paid to fostering civic virtue, which Anti-Federalists insist must be more vigorously cultivated in the populace.

### Essential Reading:

"Brutus," Second Essay; in Storing, *The Complete Anti-Federalist*, Vol. 2, pp. 372–77. "The Federal Farmer," 16th Letter; in Storing, *The Complete Anti-Federalist*, Vol. 2, pp. 323–30.

*The Federalist*, Paper 84.

The Virginia Declaration of Rights.

### Supplementary Reading:

Goldwin, *From Parchment to Power*, Part 2.

Storing, *What the Anti-Federalists Were For*, Chapters 8 and 9.

### Questions to Consider:

**1.** What do you find to be the strongest of the Federalist arguments against a Bill of Rights—and what is the best Anti-Federalist response?

**2.** How does the argument over the Bill of Rights bring out the fundamental strengths and weaknesses of each side in the Great Debate?

# Lecture Twelve—Transcript
## The Bill of Rights

Throughout the Great Debate, a leading feature of the Anti-Federalists' critique of the proposed constitution is their complaint about the absence of a Bill of Rights or—and this becomes more pronounced as the debate goes on and the Anti-Federalists see that they are losing because states are ratifying—their insistence that a Bill of Rights must be added, in amendments to the proposed constitution. It was in this dimension of their critique that they, of course, eventually tasted victory and made their most famous and massively significant contribution to the Constitution and to our whole political tradition, with the significant help of Thomas Jefferson and other figures who supported ratifying the proposed constitution, but agreed with this part of the Anti-Federalist criticism of the proposed constitution.

Yet, as we shall see, this victory was not as substantial as it had first seemed, and even such as it was, it was bittersweet, because the Bill of Rights that was added, by way of amendments drawn up in the First Congress under the guidance of James Madison, did not alter anything important in the proposed constitution. The Bill of Rights that Madison designed, in fact, strengthened the new Constitution in significant ways, and even gave to the central government, and especially to the federal judiciary, some important additional power, contrary to the wish and intention of the Anti-Federalists in their agitation for a Bill of Rights. So there is considerable irony in this Anti-Federalist "victory."

The agitation for a Bill of Rights began in the closing days of the convention itself. Starting on August 20, with a proposal by Charles Pinckney of South Carolina, it had been decided to insert into relevant sections of the Constitution statements of certain basic rights: the guarantee of the writ of habeas corpus, as well as trial by jury in criminal cases, together with prohibitions on religious tests for office, on ex post facto laws and bills of attainder. Pinckney had urged unsuccessfully that a guarantee of freedom of the press also be inserted.

On September 12, when the convention was about to conclude its business, George Mason expressed his deep dismay that there was not a formal Bill of Rights at the head of the proposed constitution and Elbridge Gerry, a leading delegate from Massachusetts, moved with Mason's second, that a Bill of Rights be drawn up.

Both of these important figures, Mason and Gerry, had already made plain their intention to oppose ratification of the Constitution. This helps explain the strange reaction of the rest of the delegates to their proposal. The motion was unanimously voted down by all the delegations from the ten states that were still present. What is still more surprising, there wasn't even any prolonged discussion giving the reasons for the rejection of a Bill of Rights. So, we're left to surmise what might have been the reasons for this rejection. Some scholars have surmised that it was felt that this would open up a large new field of difficulties and controversies, just when the tired delegates were concluding their long and arduous task rife with delicate compromises.

The problem with this explanation is that Mason had suggested that, in his words, "with the aid of the state declarations, a bill might be prepared in a few hours." Mason was referring to the fact that eight of the states had existing bills of rights, which closely resembled one another, because all were modeled on the great Virginia Declaration of Rights, which had been crafted by Mason himself. So Mason is on very strong ground when he implies that a template already existed, and that he, as the genius behind that template, could have easily drawn up a national adaptation of it.

It seems that it was rather something deeply troubling about the idea of such a declaration of rights that moved the convention to refuse to even consider it. What were the serious reasons why the idea of a declaration of rights was so troubling? Why did the Federalists come around to the idea only gradually and reluctantly?

The reasons become clearer when we consider how the agitation for a Bill of Rights played out in the subsequent ratification debates. For this agitation was seen, by both sides, as part of the broader effort by the Anti-Federalists to require amendments that would decisively weaken the proposed central government. It was part of the Anti-Federalist campaign to weaken, also, the people's trust in the proposed central government. The Anti-Federalists, in line with their strong distrust of the oligarchic tendencies of all government that was not local and close to the people, thought that it was a healthy thing to inspire the people with vigilance against, and even some distrust of, this new central government.

This goes with the specific content of the Bill of Rights as envisaged by the Anti-Federalists and also by Thomas Jefferson. Because the Anti-Federalists have in mind something like what was found in the state bills of rights, the paradigm being the Virginia Declaration. These state bills of rights, which were a legacy of the revolutionary period, were themselves revolutionary and radical documents. They included broad statements of political philosophy, elaborating the basic principles of justice and of legitimate government, based on the sovereignty of the people, expressed in the ideas of natural rights, the state of nature, the social contract and stressing the people's right of revolutionary resistance to government when it becomes oppressive.

These declarations of basic principles of political philosophy were a legacy of the struggle against English domination and also of the earlier struggle, within England, against the oppressive prerogatives of the monarchy. These declarations breathed the spirit of distrust of government that was characteristic of the revolutionary period and movement. The Anti-Federalists, to some extent, hope to transfer that spirit to the people's outlook on this new national government.

The Anti-Federalists also stress the need for such solemn declarations as means of educating the people in their civic principles, rights, and duties. In other words, they have in mind declarations that would be declarations of duties as well as rights and that would include strong exhortations to civic virtue, and even to religious piety, embodying an echo of the classical republican concern for popular virtue as a bulwark of freedom.

Thus, to take the paradigmatic example, the Virginia Declaration of Rights concludes with the following provisions:

> That no free government, or the blessings of liberty, can be preserved to any people but by a firm adherence to justice, moderation, temperance, frugality, and virtue; and by frequent recurrence to fundamental principles. That religion, or the duty which we owe to our Creator and the manner of discharging it, can be directed by reason and conviction, not by force or violence; and therefore, all men are equally entitled to the free exercise of religion, according to the dictates of conscience; and that it is the mutual duty of all to practice Christian forbearance, love, and charity towards each other.

It's in this context of the idea of broad statements, of basic republican principles and of moral virtues and of civic and religious duties, that the state declarations also enumerate basic inalienable rights and freedoms of the populace and of individuals, which the central government or in the case of the states, the state governments, are explicitly required to preserve and respect as sacrosanct; in particular, freedom of the press, freedom of religion and conscience, and basic common law procedural rights in civil and criminal law. The Anti-Federalists have something similar in mind to this sort of package for their proposed Bill of Rights.

Finally and most troubling of all for the Federalists, Jefferson, as well as the Anti-Federalists, want to include in the declaration of rights, specific and far-reaching prohibitions on what the central government can do. In particular, they want some sort of prohibition on a professional army in peacetime and a strong statement affirming the state militias as the backbone of the nation's defense. They want, in addition, explicit limitations on the national government's powers to tax and explicit limitations on the power of the central government to regulate the economy. In particular, Jefferson and the Anti-Federalists called for a prohibition of any government-established monopolies, which would, of course, have gravely limited the possibility of any public utilities under the national government, and they also want strong affirmations of states' rights and state prerogatives. In short, Jefferson and the Anti-Federalists hope, through the vehicle of a Bill of Rights, to win some of the restrictions they wish to see put on this central government's powers.

Especially when we see this last aspect of what Jefferson and the Anti-Federalists had in mind, we can better understand what is probably the most important reason why the Federalists were so troubled by the proposal for a Bill of Rights. Because the Federalists quite rightly saw that the agitation for a Bill of Rights was a part of a larger movement aimed at weakening or frustrating the Constitution's forging of a powerful central government.

In addition to this grave concern, the Federalists, including Madison, also had some other arguments expressing serious worries in principle about the effect of a Bill of Rights, some of which are laid out in Hamilton's *Federalist* Paper 84. The primary argument of the Federalists is that a Bill of Rights is not necessary. Historically, as Hamilton stresses, bills of rights have been needed to restrict or deny the traditional, oppressive, feudal claims of monarchic, unrepresentative government—divine right of kings and so on. But, Hamilton protests, we no longer face such a government as we did face when we were ruled by and struggling against the British. As Hamilton puts it in Paper 84:

> It is evident, therefore, that according to their primitive signification, [bills of rights] have no application to constitutions professedly founded upon the power of the people, and executed by their immediate representatives and servants. Here, in strictness,

the people surrender nothing, and as they retain everything, they have no need of particular reservations.

Besides, Hamilton argues, it's not words on paper that really protect rights, it's the proper design of the Constitution, creating a government that truly represents the people, that is energetic enough to protect rights, and that is safely checked and balanced from within. We have created such a government and as Hamilton says, "The truth is, after all the declamation we have heard, that the Constitution is itself, in every rational sense, and to every useful purpose, a Bill of Rights."

The Federalists argue that a Bill of Rights is not only unnecessary, but would be in crucial respects risky, because, they say, to lay down a list of rights that limit the government would carry the dangerous implication that the government would otherwise, without the list, have the power to infringe those rights. But our whole constitutional system, Hamilton argues, is based on the principle, that all rights and powers not explicitly given to the government by the Constitution are kept by the people. This is reinforced by the fact that the powers granted to the national legislature in this Constitution are enumerated powers; there is no blanket grant of power.

In addition, the Federalists warn, to this dangerous implication of a Bill of Rights that, if these rights weren't in a bill the government would somehow have the right, for example, to regulate freedom of the press, in addition, the Federalists warn, if you compose an official listing of the basic rights, it will be impossible to get on that list all the basic rights or to encompass the full meaning of all the basic rights, with all their implications. You know what's going to happen, Hamilton says, any rights that aren't on the list, future generations will say aren't protected by the Constitution because they're not in the Bill of Rights. So what you're going to do is put our rights in a straightjacket, Hamilton says, you're going to make up a list and then anything not on that list, 50 years from now judges will say, "Well, I can't find it in the Bill of Rights, so it's not protected. It's not a constitutional right." That goes against the whole purpose of our Constitution, which is to protect rights in a generous, broad way, to protect all rights, to protect rights that maybe we can't think of right now. As James Wilson said at the Pennsylvania Ratifying Convention:

> If we attempt an enumeration, everything that is not enumerated is presumed to be given up to the government. The consequence is that an imperfect enumeration would throw all implied power into the scale of the government, and the rights of the people would be

rendered incomplete. ... I consider [he says] that there are very few who understand the whole of these rights. All the political writers, from Grotius and Pufendorf, down to Vattel, have treated on this subject; but in no one of those books, nor in the aggregate of them, can you find a complete enumeration of rights appertaining to the people as men and as citizens.

As Madison put it in a private letter to Jefferson:

There's great reason [he writes to Jefferson] to fear that a positive declaration of some of the most essential rights could not be obtained in the requisite latitude. I am sure that the rights of conscience in particular, if submitted to public definition, would be narrowed much more than they are likely ever to be by an assumed power.

In other words, another problem, Madison is saying, is that if you ask people today what are the rights of conscience, you're not going to get a full enough expression. It's safer, the Federalists argue, to leave the rights unlisted, to be invoked and articulated over time as occasion calls for by the people and government officials including, especially, the judges and courts. Rights are guaranteed in an effective way, they argued, not by being listed in a document, but by being treasured in the hearts and practices of the people and their representatives and judges. Hamilton writes,

What signifies a declaration, that, for example, "the liberty of the press shall be inviolably preserved"? What is the liberty of the press? Who can give it any definition [that] would not leave the utmost latitude for evasion? I hold it to be impracticable; and from this I infer, that its security, whatever fine declarations may be inserted in any constitution respecting it, must altogether depend on public opinion, and on the general spirit of the people and of the government.

Precisely to this point, the Anti-Federalists have a powerful response together with Jefferson, who argued this strongly to Madison. They argue for the civic educational importance of a permanent, enshrined documentary statement of the most important basic rights, which they say can include some general cautionary provision at the end, some statement to the effect that there are many other rights that are not here enumerated, that are reserved to the people and to the states and so on. In other words, they say, you don't have to say just these are the rights, you can add something to the effect, these are the most important rights, but not all of them. The key point is we need a statement in this document to remind people what it's all for and about. As "The Federal Farmer" eloquently puts it in his 16th letter:

> We do not by declarations change the nature of things, or create new truths, but we give existence, or at least establish, in the minds of the people, truths and principles which they might never otherwise have thought of, or soon forgot … What is the usefulness of a truth in theory, unless it exists constantly in the minds of the people, and has their assent … it is the effect of education, a series of notions impressed upon the minds of the people by examples, precepts, and declarations.

As Edmund Randolph, the governor of Virginia, said of the function of the Virginia Declaration of Rights, it was, he says, to "lay the corner stone, on which a constitution was to be raised" by making it so that "in all the revolutions of time, of human opinion, and of government, a perpetual standard should be erected around which the people might rally, and by a notorious record to be forever admonished to be watchful, firm, and virtuous."

This consideration, the civic educational value for the people at large in the future of a Bill of Rights, played a major role in gradually winning James Madison over to Jefferson's point of view.

What actually happened to bring about the amendments that constitute our Bill of Rights as we have them was that many of the Federalists, and above all, James Madison, became persuaded, in the course of the debate, that if the statement of rights were properly and carefully crafted, a big if, then such a statement would do more good than harm.

In part, Madison was moved by a major political consideration, too. He recognized that in the wake of the Great Debate, when the Constitution had been ratified and the First Congress was starting to meet, that although the Constitution had been ratified and was up and going, there was a widespread opposition still and distrust and doubt about it amongst that sizable part of the population, and it might even have been a majority, who had supported the Anti-Federalist side or at least been impressed by their arguments. The clearest manifestation of this was the fact that a large number of amendments had been recommended by the various state ratifying conventions. So while the Constitution had been ratified in most of the states, it was only with a big list of amendments that were wanted, many of which included bills of rights. So Madison calculated, as a politician, that if there were added a Bill of Rights whose language was crafted in such a way that it did not weaken the new government and did not foster distrust of the new government and did not stress and thus arouse the people's right of resistance to government, then such an addition of a moderated version of a Bill of Rights would go a long way in mollifying and reassuring and reconciling the opponents.

So to the crafting of such a Bill of Rights Madison devoted his great talents, leading the First Congress in this activity. The Bill of Rights as it emerged from that Congress omitted most of what the Anti-Federalists had hoped would be included. Madison did use the amendments, and above all the First Amendment, as a forum for expressing and teaching succinctly certain very fundamental rights, freedom of speech and religion and of the press, and then later key property rights and key procedural rights in criminal and civil law. But Madison omitted all language that would tie those rights to any specific political philosophy. He left out any reference to natural rights or the state of nature, or the social compact, all the key philosophic conceptions that were prominent in the state declarations, and he left out all reference to cultivating civic virtue and piety, the echoes of classical republicanism that the Anti-Federalists wanted.

Madison fended off a strong effort by some leading figures in the Congress, especially Elbridge Gerry and other Anti-Federalist congressmen, who wanted to consider the kind of Bill of Rights they wanted. The result was that some of these die-hard Anti-Federalists were furious and disgusted with the actual Bill of Rights that was adopted. By thus keeping the Constitution's Bill of Rights detached from any specific philosophic or theological grounding, Madison facilitated popular reverence for and attachment to the Constitution itself, for its own sake or as a kind of self-sufficient object of reverence, not referring back to revolutionary principles on the basis of which the people are encouraged to doubt or resist or question their constitution and constitutional government.

In other words, where the Anti-Federalists had tended to want a Bill of Rights that taught people to look at the federal government and maybe even the Constitution with a skeptical eye, possibly as a potential threat to their basic rights, Madison led the way in formulating a Bill of Rights that reassured people of their rights being respected and protected by the federal government, especially since the federal judiciary was now able to appeal to the Bill of Rights in their exercise of judicial review.

This fits with and expresses Madison's and the Federalists' overwhelming priority, which was not the Bill of Rights, which Madison saw as at best a secondary support and clarification of what it was that the constitutional government was designed to protect. No, the key thing for Madison and the Federalists was the Constitution itself, the body of the Constitution, and the wonderful design and frame of government that it invites.

So one can say that the Bill of Rights as we have it is not so much the product of the Anti-Federalist agitation as it is rather the product of James Madison's fundamental re-crafting of the Anti-Federalist idea. As Madison himself put it, in his great speech advancing the Bill of Rights in the First Congress on June 8, 1789,

> It has been a fortunate thing [he says] that the objection to the Government has been made on the ground I stated [of a Bill of Rights]; because it will be practicable, on that ground, to obviate the objection, so far as to satisfy the public mind that their liberties will be perpetual, and this without endangering any part of the Constitution, which is considered as essential to the existence of the Government by those who promoted its adoption.

It's especially fitting for us to conclude our study with the debate over the Bill of Rights, because in that debate are expressed some of the major strengths and weaknesses and the most important legacy of each side. The Federalists deservedly won the Great Debate, because they successfully defended a marvelously well-designed frame of governmental power, while the Anti-Federalists deservedly lost because they lacked a convincing alternative proposal.

The Anti-Federalists, in their losing critique, show us some real limits of the magnificent proposal. They help us to see what has had to be left out or left behind, especially of the classical tradition, and they alert us to some dangers that lurk in this new order, as a result. The Anti-Federalists, together with Jefferson—and many of the Anti-Federalists became followers of Jefferson in the Great Party Divide that shook the nation after the Constitution—they were the first to voice in a serious way a set of worries that have played a healthy critical role in our civic tradition.

They warn of a tendency in large-scale, centralized government, even though it is representative, to become oppressive by losing touch with the real lives and concerns of the people by becoming intrusive, paternalistic, bureaucratic, by reducing citizens to child-like passivity and dependence, thus sapping the energy and dulling the capacities of citizens to become engaged in self-government and to take individual and collective responsibility for their lives. The Anti-Federalists plead eloquently for the spiritual value of strong local institutions that foster direct popular participation in self-government.

The Anti-Federalists do seem to have been overly distrustful of strong central government, too suspicious of the oligarchic tendencies of government removed from the people. The Anti-Federalists seem to fail to appreciate how skillfully the Constitution was designed to achieve a central government that was both energetic and safe, and well-checked and balanced. On the other hand, the Anti-Federalists expressed what was to become widespread dissatisfaction at the insufficient amount of direct popular control over and involvement in the choice of the national government. The Anti-Federalists rightly saw that this original Constitution was insufficiently democratic or populist to fit the character and expectations of a people like the Americans.

Thus, the electoral college as a method of selecting the President never worked as planned, because it met with popular resistance from the start. The electoral college became almost at once merely a somewhat bizarre system for expressing popular majorities or pluralities in Presidential elections. Mass political parties soon formed, which have ever since played an enormous but extra-constitutional role in American politics, enabling much greater mass involvement in politics and the choice of national officers. The Senate eventually became much more democratically elected and a much less aristocratic body than the Federalists planned.

The deepest and perhaps the most important Anti-Federalist contribution is their highlighting of the insufficient attention paid by the founders and by our Constitution to fostering civic virtue through civic education, encouraging civic citizen participation; all of which, the Anti-Federalists plausibly insist and fruitfully warn, must be more vigorously cultivated in the populace if our system is not going to drift slowly toward a condition in which a passive, apathetic, and atomized populace becomes dominated by a paternalistic, bureaucratic, and distant government apparatus.

The kind of civic education the Anti-Federalists warn us that we need to keep striving to invigorate includes, as an important cornerstone, what we have been doing in this course itself: the ever-renewed rethinking of the Great Debate out of which our unique republic was born.

# Timeline

1748 .............................................. Montesquieu's *Spirit of the Laws*
published (English translation 1750).

1774

September 5 .................................... First Continental Congress at
Philadelphia.

1775

April 19........................................... Battles of Lexington and Concord begin
the American Revolution.

1776

June 12............................................ Virginia Declaration of Rights (written
by George Mason) adopted.

July 4.............................................. Declaration of Independence approved.

1777

November 15................................... Articles of Confederation passed by
Continental Congress.

1781

March 1 .......................................... Articles of Confederation go into force
after being ratified by the last of the 13
states.

1783

September 3 .................................... Treaty of Paris ends the Revolutionary
War.

1786

August 29........................................ Shays' Rebellion begins in
Massachusetts (put down by force
February 3, 1787).

1787

May 25 ............................................ Federal Convention begins in
Philadelphia.

September 17 ................................. Proposed constitution signed and sent to the states for ratification.

September 27 ................................. Publication of first of the Anti-Federalist *Letters of Cato* (probably by Governor George Clinton of New York).

October 5 ..................................... Publication of the first of the Anti-Federalist *Letters of Centinel* (by Samuel Bryan, with the collaboration of his father, Judge George Bryan).

mid-October .................................. Anti-Federalist *Letters from The Federal Farmer* (probably written by Richard Henry Lee) begin to appear, the first dated October 8 (despite being dated October 8, *Federal Farmer* is thought to have actually come out in November); Anti-Federalist "Essays of Brutus" (probably written by Robert Yates) begin to appear, the first dated October 18.

October 27 .................................... *The Federalist*, by Hamilton, Madison, and Jay, begins to appear under the pen name "Publius."

November 22 ................................. George Mason's formal objections to the proposed constitution published.

December 7 ................................... Delaware's convention ratifies the constitution by unanimous vote.

December 10 ................................. Publication of Edmund Randolph's letter detailing his objections.

December 12 ................................. Pennsylvania's convention ratifies by a vote of 46 to 23, with bitter minority opposition and an important speech in favor of the constitution by James Wilson.

| | |
|---|---|
| December 18 .................................. | New Jersey's convention ratifies unanimously. |
| December 21 .................................. | Robert Yates and John Lansing send to Governor Clinton of New York their formal objections. |
| December 31 .................................. | Georgia's convention ratifies unanimously. |

1788

| | |
|---|---|
| January 9 ....................................... | Connecticut's convention ratifies by 128–40. |
| January 27 ..................................... | Luther Martin sends his lengthy formal objections to the Maryland House of Delegates. |
| February 6 ..................................... | Massachusetts's convention ratifies after a long debate by 187–168, with the recommendation of numerous substantial amendments to be made by the first Congress. |
| March 22 ....................................... | First 36 *Federalist* papers published as a bound volume in New York by J. McLean and Co. ("The McLean Edition"). |
| April 28 ......................................... | Maryland's convention ratifies by 63–11. |
| May 23 .......................................... | South Carolina's convention ratifies by 149–73. |
| May 28 .......................................... | Remaining *Federalist* papers (37 through 85) published in a second volume ("The McLean Edition"). |
| June 21 .......................................... | New Hampshire's convention ratifies, after a long debate, by 57–47, with a call for numerous substantial amendments to be made by the first Congress; as the ninth state, it |

completes the minimum necessary for the Constitution to become law.

June 25 ........................................... Virginia's convention ratifies, after long debate, by 89–79, with a call for numerous substantial amendments to be made by the first Congress.

July 26 ........................................... New York's convention ratifies, after long debate, by 30–27, with a call for numerous substantial amendments to be made by the first Congress.

August 2 ........................................ North Carolina's convention refuses to ratify by 184–83.

September 13 ................................. Resolution of the Congress Fixing Date for Election of a President, and the Organization of the Government under the Constitution, in the City of New York.

1789

March 4 .......................................... Resolution of the First Congress Submitting Twelve Amendments to the Constitution (the Bill of Rights).

November 21 ................................. North Carolina holds a second convention, which ratifies by 194–77.

1790

May 29 ........................................... Rhode Island's convention ratifies by 34–32 (after having ratification defeated in a popular referendum by 2,708–237).

1792 ............................................... French translation of *The Federalist Papers*, the first to reveal the authors' names, published in Paris.

1805 ............................................... Anti-Federalist Mercy Otis Warren publishes her *History of the Rise, Progress, and Termination of the American Revolution*.

# Glossary

**Anti-Federalists:** The term designating those who opposed ratification of the proposed constitution of 1787.

**aristocracy:** From the ancient Greek meaning, literally, "rule by the best." A government in which the decisive power is in the hands of a minority qualified by its virtue or excellence.

**checks and balances:** Any of a wide range of constitutional and institutional ways of dividing and counterbalancing power of government in order to prevent its consolidation into potentially despotic authority.

**classical republicanism:** Deriving from ancient Greece, the tradition, in theory and in practice, of self-government that stresses direct citizen participation and the need for citizen virtue.

**confederacy, federation, confederation:** Terms designating an association of independent republics who have joined to form a permanent union under a central government without dissolving or merging the members and their distinct governments, which retain some substantial degree of sovereignty.

**democracy:** From the ancient Greek meaning literally "rule by the multitude." A government in which the decisive power is in the hands of the majority of the citizens.

**federalism:** A term designating the theory and practice of confederacies.

**Federalists:** The term designating those who supported ratification of the proposed constitution of 1787 without any substantial amendments.

**judicial review:** The theory and practice whereby the judiciary (and above all the Supreme Court) has the duty and right to invalidate otherwise proper legislation on the grounds that, in the judges' view, it contradicts the Constitution as the fundamental and preeminent law.

**militia:** A military composed of citizens serving part-time—in contrast to a "standing army."

**mixed regime:** A government, favored as the best in practice by the classical republican tradition, that combines major elements of democracy, aristocracy, and monarchy in order to elicit the virtues and mitigate the vices of each of the three forms.

**separation of powers:** The theory and practice whereby no two of what are understood to be the distinct functional powers of government are placed in the same hands. In its fully developed form, articulated above all by Montesquieu, it means that no two of the legislative, executive, and judiciary powers should be vested in the same hands.

**Shays' Rebellion:** An armed uprising in western Massachusetts that started on August 29, 1786, in which small farmers—angered by crushing debt and taxes and led by Daniel Shays (a decorated and distinguished captain in the Revolution)—sought to close local courts enforcing judgments against them. A Massachusetts militia that had been raised as a private army easily defeated the main Shaysite force on February 3, 1787; the uprising, however, gravely alarmed people throughout the 13 states as a sign of rising anarchy and was used as a frightening harbinger by proponents of a new constitution.

**standing army:** A professional, full-time military—in contrast to a part-time, citizen militia.

**yeomanry:** The class of small farmers who possess and work enough land of their own to give them economic independence; a member of this class is called a yeoman.

# Biographical Notes

Note: The authors of *The Federalist*—Hamilton, Madison, and Jay—published under the pen name of "**Publius**." Anti-Federalist pen names included "**Agrippa**" (James Winthrop), "**Brutus**" (probably Robert Yates), "**Candidus**" (Samuel Adams or his follower Benjamin Austin), "**Cato**" (probably George Clinton), "**Centinel**" (Samuel Bryan), "**Cincinnatus**" (perhaps Arthur Lee, brother of Richard Henry Lee), "**The Federal Farmer**" (Richard Henry Lee), "**A [Pennsylvania] Farmer**" (unknown), and "**Plebian**" (Melancton Smith).

**Adams, Samuel** (1722–1803). Revolutionary leader in Boston, delegate to the Continental Congress, and signer of the Declaration of Independence. A leading delegate at the Massachusetts ratifying convention and a critic of the proposed constitution, he and John Hancock led the effort at compromise by which the Constitution was approved—but with numerous substantial amendments recommended to the first Congress. Either he or a follower of his named Benjamin Austin authored the Anti-Federalist "Essays by Candidus."

**"Agrippa."** The pen name taken by James Winthrop in writing an important series of Massachusetts Anti-Federalist essays. The name evokes a number of figures of that name in Roman history.

**Aristotle** (384–322 B.C.). Student of Plato and author of numerous independent seminal and foundational philosophic works. His treatises in moral and political philosophy, especially *Politics* and *Ethics*, are the fountainheads of classical republican political theory in its original form.

**"Brutus."** The pen name adopted by the author (probably Robert Yates) of one of the most important sets of Anti-Federalist essays. The name evokes the legendary Lucius Junius Brutus (c. 500 B.C.), leader in the expulsion of the kings from Rome and originator of the Consular Constitution of the Republic. Brutus died in the battle that defeated the last king in his attempt to return to power; Publius Valerius Publicola was his partner who survived him to lead the republic (see "Publius").

**Bryan, Samuel** (precise dates unknown). Author of the "Letters of Centinel," one of the most important of the Anti-Federalist writings. Son of George Bryan, a prominent Pennsylvania legislator and judge, who was the principal leader of the Anti-Federalists in that state and who probably collaborated closely in the writing.

**"Candidus."** The pen name (Latin for "candid") adopted by the author of a series of prominent Massachusetts Anti-Federalist essays, written either by Samuel Adams or a follower of his named Benjamin Austin.

**"Cato."** The pen name adopted by the author (probably George Clinton) of a major series of Anti-Federalist essays published in New York. The name evokes two Roman heroes: Cato the Elder (234–149 B.C.), a severe censor of morals and opponent of corruption in the republic; and his great-grandson, Cato the Younger (95–46 B.C.), a Stoic paradigm who committed suicide after vainly attempting to defend the republic against its overthrow by Julius Caesar. Cato the Younger was the subject of Joseph Addison's tragedy *Cato* (1712), which was extremely popular among Americans in the Revolutionary and founding period.

**"Centinel."** The pen name adopted by Samuel Bryan for a major series of Pennsylvania Anti-Federalist essays.

**Chase, Samuel** (1741–1811). Revolutionary leader in Maryland, where he led the agitation in support of the Declaration of Independence (of which he was a signer as delegate to the Continental Congress). A delegate to the Maryland ratifying convention, he delivered speeches thoughtfully critical of the constitution, the notes for which survive.

**"Cincinnatus."** The pen name adopted by the unknown author of a series of New York Anti-Federalist essays. The name evokes a legendary hero of the Roman republic who twice was called from his humble farm to become temporary dictator and each time saved the republic from enemies both internal and external.

**Clinton, George** (1739–1812). A revolutionary leader who was a delegate to the Continental Congress, a general in the Continental army, and governor of New York (1777–1795 and 1801–1804); at the time of the Constitutional Convention, he was the most powerful man in New York. He led the opposition to the proposed constitution, wrote an important set of essays under the pen name "Cato," and delivered speeches in the ratifying convention. He became Vice President under Thomas Jefferson and then again under James Madison; he died during the latter's administration.

**"Cornelius."** The pen name adopted by the unknown author of a Massachusetts Anti-Federalist essay that is among the few that originated from outside of Boston. The name evokes a Roman tribal surname.

**"De Witt, John."** The pen name adopted by the unknown author of a set of intelligent Boston Anti-Federalist essays; the name is likely meant to evoke Jan De Witt, the great leader of the Dutch republican movement.

**"Federal Farmer, The."** A pen name adopted by the author (probably Richard Henry Lee) of one of the most important series of Anti-Federalist writings.

**Gerry, Elbridge** (1744–1813). A young leader of the Revolution in Massachusetts, a delegate to the Continental Congress, and a signer of the Declaration of Independence and the Articles of Confederation. He was an active and outspoken delegate to the Constitutional Convention and in the end declared himself a strong opponent of the product and of its ratification. He later became governor of Massachusetts and succeeded George Clinton as Vice President under Madison, then died in office.

**Hamilton, Alexander** (1755–1804). Chief staff aide to Washington and commander of fighting forces in the Revolution, he was the leader of the effort that led to the Constitutional Convention. Perhaps his greatest achievement was the organizing and authorship of two-thirds of *The Federalist*. Rivaling this was his service as the first treasury secretary of the United States, where he proved himself a brilliant economist and visionary promulgator of public policies of finance and economic planning.

**Hancock, John** (1737–1793). Revolutionary leader in Massachusetts, delegate to the Continental Congress, and first signer of the Declaration of Independence. As first governor of Massachusetts, he served nine terms; he also presided over the Massachusetts ratification convention. A critic of the proposed constitution, he led, together with Samuel Adams, the effort at compromise by which Massachusetts approved the constitution but with numerous substantial amendments recommended to the first Congress.

**Henry, Patrick** (1736–1799). A brilliant orator and leader (four-term governor) of Virginia in the Revolution, he spoke with his characteristic rolling and electrifying eloquence against the constitution in the Virginia ratifying convention. He accepted the defeat of his cause gracefully, though, and was asked by Washington in 1795 to be secretary of state (which he declined).

**Jay, John** (1745–1829). The youngest member of the Continental Congress and a leading figure in New York politics, where he drafted the first state constitution and was appointed chief justice of the State Supreme Court. Subsequently he served as one of America's preeminent ambassadors and was the first chief justice of the United States Supreme Court. He was one of the three authors of *The Federalist*, though prevented by a wound from writing more than five of the papers; he also wrote a separate essay in defense of the constitution and was an outspoken Federalist delegate to the New York ratifying convention.

**Jefferson, Thomas** (1743–1826). Author of the Declaration of Independence and third President of the United States. He was abroad at the time of the Constitutional Convention and the debates over ratification. Under the influence of his close friend Madison, he was won over from skepticism to a somewhat reluctant support of the proposed constitution—though insisting on the addition of a Bill of Rights.

**Lansing, John** (1754–1829). Speaker of the Assembly of New York and delegate to the Constitutional Convention as a follower of Governor Clinton, he walked out with his colleague Robert Yates after six weeks and became an outspoken opponent of ratification, especially in the New York convention.

**Lee, Richard Henry** (1732–1794). A leader in the Revolution and among the delegates in the Continental Congress, he first moved and spoke for a Declaration of Independence. President of the Congress at the time of the calling of the Constitutional Convention, he opposed ratification of the proposed constitution except on the condition of very substantial amendments. He is the probable author of one of the most significant Anti-Federalist writings, *Letters from the Federal Farmer*.

**Madison, James** (1751–1836). A leader in the Constitutional Convention, in the Virginia ratifying convention, and in the first United States Congress, where he orchestrated the drawing up and passage of the Bill of Rights. He authored about one-third of *The Federalist* and was later fourth President of the United States.

**Martin, Luther** (1748–1826). A revolutionary leader in Maryland, a brilliantly successful lawyer, and attorney general of Maryland for 32 years. As a delegate to the Constitutional Convention, he was from his arrival a strong and outspoken dissenter. He finally walked out with John Francis Mercer and wrote and spoke vigorously in opposition to ratification.

**"[Maryland] Farmer, The."** The pen name adopted by John Francis Mercer in writing several intelligent critiques of the proposed constitution.

**Mason, George** (1725–1792). A leader of the Revolution in Virginia and author of both the Virginia Constitution and Declaration of Rights. As delegate to the Constitutional Convention, he was outspoken, arguing among other things against slavery and in favor of a Bill of Rights; he eventually declared his strong opposition to the finished product—which he criticized in a published statement and in speeches as a delegate to the Virginia ratifying convention.

**Mercer, John Francis** (1759–1821). The second youngest delegate to the Constitutional Convention, at the age of 28. From Maryland, he walked out of the proceedings together with Luther Martin and subsequently authored and coauthored several intelligent critiques of the proposed constitution, including one under the pen name of "A [Maryland] Farmer." Later a congressman and two-term governor of Maryland.

**Monroe, James** (1758–1831). At the time of the Constitutional Convention, he was a young rising star in Virginia politics. Though strongly nationalist, he had serious objections to the proposed constitution and wrote (but never published) an essay elaborating them; he was later fifth President of the United States.

**Montesquieu, Charles-Louis de Secondat, Baron de** (1689–1755). The most authoritative political philosopher for Americans during the founding period on account of his massive treatise, *The Spirit of the Laws* (1748; English translation 1750), with its great themes of democracy grounded on virtue, federalism, separation of powers, judicial protection of individual liberty, and the liberating effect of commercialism.

**"[Pennsylvania] Farmer, A."** The pen name adopted by the unknown author of an intelligent Anti-Federalist essay, "The Fallacies of a Freeman Detected by a Farmer."

**Plato** (c. 421–341 B.C.). Greek philosopher, student of Socrates, and teacher of Aristotle, his dialogues are the chief fountainhead of subsequent Western philosophy and classical republican political theory.

**Plutarch** (c. A.D. 46–127). Greek historian and philosophic writer who flourished under the Roman emperors Hadrian and Trajan. Most famous for his *Lives of Famous Greeks and Romans*, which was widely read and cited during the founding period.

**"Publius."** The pen name chosen by the authors of *The Federalist*, evoking Publius Valerius Publicola (c. 500), the partner of Lucius Junius Brutus in the expulsion of the kings from Rome and the founding of the republic. Brutus died in the battle defeating the last king's attempt to return, and Publius was left to lead the new republic. Publius is the subject of one of Plutarch's biographies.

**Randolph, Edmund** (1753–1813). Governor of Virginia at the time of the Constitutional Convention and a very active and constructive delegate at the convention itself, he nonetheless refused to sign in the end and wrote an ambiguous explanation of his decision. At the Virginia ratifying convention, he turned to supporting ratification. Washington later appointed him the first attorney general of the United States and subsequently secretary of state.

**"Samuel."** The pen name, evoking the biblical prophet, adopted by the unknown author of a Boston Anti-Federalist essay.

**Shays, Daniel** (c. 1747–1825). A decorated and distinguished captain in the Revolution, he became famous as the leader of "Shays' Rebellion"—an armed uprising in western Massachusetts that started on August 29, 1786, in which small farmers angered by crushing debt and taxes sought to close local courts enforcing judgments against them (see Glossary).

**Smith, Melancton** (1744–1798). A veteran of the Revolution and a delegate to the Continental Congress (1785–1787), he was a leading delegate to the New York state ratifying convention and an articulate speaker against the proposed constitution, debating with Alexander Hamilton.

**Warren, Mercy Otis** (1728–1814). Author of patriotic plays and poetry during the Revolution, of which she wrote an elaborate history published in 1805. She is the author of a major Anti-Federalist essay under the pen name of "A Columbian Patriot."

**Winthrop, James** (1752–1821). A veteran of the Revolution and of the militia force that suppressed Shays' Rebellion, he was a librarian at Harvard, a Massachusetts judge, and the author of an intelligent series of Anti-Federalist essays under the pen name "Agrippa."

**Yates, Robert** (1738–1801). Appointed to the New York Supreme Court in 1777 and eventually chief justice (1790–1798). A delegate to the Constitutional Convention, Yates walked out early with his colleague John

Lansing and attacked the finished product not only in his role as a delegate to the state ratifying convention but as the probable author of a series of essays by "Brutus" that are among the greatest Anti-Federalist writings.

# Bibliography

**Essential Readings:**

*The Federalist.* Edited by George W. Carey and James McClellan. Indianapolis: Liberty Fund, 2001. The best edition of the classic defense and explanation of the Founders' understanding of the American Constitution by Alexander Hamilton, John Jay, and James Madison. Available online at: http://oll.libertyfund.org/Home3/Book.php?recordID=0084.2.

Gillespie, Michael, and Michael Lienesch, eds. *Ratifying the Constitution.* Lawrence, KS: University Press of Kansas, 1989. A careful state-by-state analysis of the process of ratification of the Constitution.

Jefferson, Thomas. *Notes on the State of Virginia*, Query 17. In Philip B. Kurland and Ralph Lerner, eds., *The Founders' Constitution.* 5 vols. Chicago: University of Chicago Press, 1987, Vol. 1, Chapter 4, Number 9. Jefferson's classic statement on the need for a yeoman, agrarian citizenry.

Ketcham, Ralph, ed. *The Anti-Federalist Papers and the Constitutional Convention Debates.* New York: Signet Classics, 2003. An excellent and handy one-volume collection of many of the most relevant documents, with Anti-Federalist writings reprinted from Storing's *The Complete Anti-Federalist.*

Montesquieu. *The Spirit of the Laws.* Amherst, NY: Prometheus Books, 2002 (orig. publ. 1752); Thomas Nugent, trans. The original English translation—used by the Founders—of the most authoritative work of political theory in the age of the founding. Available online at: www.constitution.org/cm/sol.htm.

Storing, Herbert J. *The Anti-Federalist.* Chicago: University of Chicago Press, 1985. An abridgement by Murray Dry of *The Complete Anti-Federalist.*

_____. *The Complete Anti-Federalist.* 7 vols. Chicago: University of Chicago Press, 1981. The most complete and best-annotated collection of writings by opponents of the ratification of the constitution. The Virginia Declaration of Rights. Available online at: www.yale.edu/lawweb/avalon/virginia.htm.

**Supplementary Readings:**

Diamond, Martin. *As Far As Republican Principles Will Admit.* Washington: AEI Press, 1992. Out of print, but insightful analysis of the meaning of federalism for the authors of *The Federalist*. See especially Chapters 6, 7, and 9.

Epstein, David. *The Political Theory of "The Federalist."* Chicago: University of Chicago Press, 1984. The best treatment of the political theory articulated and implicit in *The Federalist*. The debate with the Anti-Federalists is deemphasized, however, and perhaps as a result, the difference between the thought of *The Federalist* and the classical republican tradition is somewhat blurred.

Goldwin, Robert A. *From Parchment to Power: How James Madison Used the Bill of Rights to Save the Constitution.* Washington: American Enterprise Institute, 1997. An excellent brief account of the forging of our Bill of Rights.

Marks, Frederick W. III. *Independence on Trial: Foreign Affairs and the Making of the Constitution.* Wilmington, DE: Scholarly Resources, 1986. The best historical account of the role of foreign affairs and arguments over national security in the founding.

Slonim, Shlomo. "Federalist no. 78 and Brutus' Neglected Thesis on Judicial Supremacy." *Constitutional Commentary* 23:1 (March 2006). A major recent recovering of the importance of the major Anti-Federalist attack on judicial review.

Storing, Herbert J. *What the Anti-Federalists Were For: The Political Thought of the Opponents of the Constitution.* Chicago: University of Chicago Press, 1981. This is a separate publication of Vol. 1 of *The Complete Anti-Federalist* (see Essential Readings). The best account of the political thought unifying the opponents of ratification of the Constitution, though the foreign and defense policy dimension of their thought is somewhat scant.

Tarcov, Nathan. "The Federalists and Anti-Federalists on Foreign Affairs." *Teaching Political Science* 14:1 (Fall 1986): 38–45. An illuminating, succinct account of the theoretical differences between Federalists and Anti-Federalists over the requirements of foreign policy.

_____. "War and Peace in *The Federalist*," *Political Science Reviewer* 19 (Spring 1990): 87–106. A more elaborate version of the preceding item.

Thatch, Charles C. *The Creation of the Presidency, 1775–1789.* Baltimore: Johns Hopkins University Press, 1969. A classic study that is especially helpful in showing the roots of the Presidency in the experience with the chief executive in the state governments.

Wirls, Daniel and Stephen. *The Invention of the United States Senate.* Baltimore: Johns Hopkins University Press, 2004. The most definitive study of the roots and evolution of the senate, with a helpful chapter on the senate in the ratification debate.

Wood, Gordon. *The Creation of the American Republic, 1776–1787.* Chapel Hill: University of North Carolina Press, 1969. A leading study that has contributed to a renewed appreciation of the thinking that animated and divided the Revolutionary and framing periods. Understands thought as "ideology" expressing social class interests; as a result, the deeper and broader theoretical dimensions of the debate among the most thoughtful leaders tend to be merged into the wider and shallower intellectual and social milieu.

**Additional Primary Sources:**

*Annals of the Congress of the United States.* Washington, DC: Gales and Seaton, 1834–1856. Contains the most complete record of the discussion in the House of Representatives concerning the formulation of the Bill of Rights. Available online at:
http://memory.loc.gov/ammem/amlaw/lwac.html.

Bailyn, Bernard, ed. *The Debate on the Constitution: Federalist and Antifederalist Speeches, Articles, and Letters During the Struggle over Ratification.* 2 vols. New York: Library of America, 1993. An extensive collection of speeches and writings on both sides of the debate.

Carey, George W., and James McClellan, eds. *The Federalist.* Indianapolis: Liberty Fund, 2001. The best edition of the classic defense and explanation of the Founders' understanding of the American Constitution by Alexander Hamilton, John Jay, and James Madison. Available online at:
http://oll.libertyfund.org/Home3/Book.php?recordID=0084.2.

Elliot, Jonathan, ed. *The Debates of the State Conventions on the Adoption of the Constitution.* 5 vols. Philadelphia: J.B. Lippincott Co., 1836 (reprinted New York: Burt Franklin, 1974). The record of the debates in each of the state ratifying conventions. Available online at:
http://memory.loc.gov/ammem/amlaw/lwed.html.

Farrand, Max, ed. *The Records of the Federal Convention of 1787.* 4 vols. New Haven: Yale University Press, 1911 (subsequent reprints). The fullest collection of records of debates in the convention and some related materials. Available online at:
http://oll.libertyfund.org/Home3/TitlesAll.php and at:
http://memory.loc.gov/ammem/amlaw/lwfr.html.

Jensen, Merrill, et al., eds. *Documentary History of the Ratification of the Constitution.* Madison: State Historical Society of Wisconsin, 1976. A comprehensive collection of documents, in a projected 29 vols. To see those published thus far, visit: http://www.wisconsinhistory.org/ratification/.

Kurland, Philip B., and Ralph Lerner, eds. *The Founders' Constitution.* 5 vols. Chicago: University of Chicago Press, 1987. A rich and intelligently selected collection of writings from before and after the founding period about every aspect of the political theory underlying the Constitution. Available online at http://press-pubs.uchicago.edu/founders/.

Schwartz, Bernard, ed. *The Roots of the Bill of Rights.* 5 vols. New York: Chelsea House, 1971. Includes documents showing the English and colonial sources of the Bill of Rights.

Sheehan, Colleen A. and Gary L. McDowell, eds. *Friends of the Constitution: Writings of the "Other" Federalists 1787–1788.* Indianapolis: Liberty Fund, 1998. A fine collection of many of the most interesting lesser Federalist writings, with an illuminating interpretative essay by Herbert J. Storing.

Tansill, Charles C., ed. *Documents Illustrative of the Formation of the Union of the American States.* Washington, DC: Government Printing Office, 1927. A widely used one-volume collection of documents relating to the Philadelphia Convention and its deliberations. Available online at: www.questia.com/library/book/documents-illustrative-of-the-formation-of-the-union-of-the-american-states-by-charles-c-tansill.jsp.

Veit, Helen, et al., eds. *Creating the Bill of Rights: The Documentary Record from the First Federal Congress.* Baltimore: Johns Hopkins University Press, 1991.

**Primary Sources on the Internet:**

Anti-Federalist Writings. An extensive collection of major Anti-Federalist writings, many complete, some excerpted (Note: The titles given to the writings on this website are not often the original titles, and the "Essays of Brutus" are misnumbered but in the correct sequential order.) http://www.infoplease.com/t/hist/antifederalist/index.html

The Avalon Project at Yale Law School. An extensive collection of documents in American history, especially from the Founding period. www.yale.edu/lawweb/avalon/avalon.htm

The Constitution Society. Contains texts of a number of major writings from the Founding period. www.constitution.org/index.shtml

Henry, Patrick. Excerpts from Speech in Virginia Ratifying Convention (June 5, 1788). Also contains other brief excerpts from Anti-Federalist authors. http://lexrex.com/enlightened/writings/liberty_empire.htm

Online Library of Liberty. A collection of numerous classic writings, including many major writings of the founding period and in particular of Anti-Federalists Richard Henry Lee and Mercy Otis Warren, as well as the works of Hamilton, Jefferson, and Washington. http://oll.libertyfund.org/Home3/TitlesAll.php

Smith, Melancton. Speeches in the New York Ratifying Convention. www.constitution.org/rc/rat_ny.htm#msmith01.

## Secondary Sources:

Bancroft, George. *History of the Formation of the Constitution of the United States of America.* 2 vols. New York: D. Appleton, 1882 (reprint Union, NJ: Lawbook Exchange, 2000). A classic study that conveys with eloquence the political and personal background but tends to underestimate the intellectual seriousness of the Anti-Federalist side. See especially Part 2, Book 4.

Beard, Charles. *An Economic Interpretation of the Constitution of the United States.* New York: Macmillan, 1913. The path-breaking attempt to interpret the thought of the founding period as largely "ideology" masking and defending the selfish class's economic interest. A telling historical critique was made by Forrest McDonald in *We the People* (see below).

Fiske, John. *The Critical Period of American History, 1783–1789.* Boston: Houghton Mifflin, 1888. A lively account that tends to glorify the Federalists at the cost of denigrating the Anti-Federalists.

McDonald, Forrest. *Novus Ordo Seclorum: The Intellectual Origins of the Constitution.* Lawrence: University Press of Kansas, 1985. Sheds important light on the English and colonial sources and roots of thinking in the founding period.

_____. *We the People: The Economic Origins of the Constitution.* Chicago: University of Chicago Press, 1958. A powerful critique of Charles Beard's economic hypothesis for explaining the thought of the founding period (see Beard).

McLaughlin, Andrew. *The Confederation and the Constitution, 1783–1789.* New York: Harper, 1905. The conventionally authoritative academic historian's account at the turn of the century. A lucid and informative, but sometimes naively patronizing, overview that favors the Federalists—

whose thought, however, is insufficiently appreciated, in large measure because of the author's belittling attitude toward the Anti-Federalists.

Rutland, Robert. *The Ordeal of the Constitution: The Antifederalists and the Ratification Struggle of 1787–1788.* Norman: University of Oklahoma Press, 1966 (reissued in 2000). A vivid narrative of the struggle over ratification as it unfolded in various key states.

# Notes

# Notes

# Notes

# Notes

# Notes

# Notes

# Notes